T0286790

Cambridge Elements

Elements in Environmental Humanities
edited by
Louise Westling
University of Oregon
Serenella Iovino
University of North Carolina at Chapel Hill
Timo Maran
University of Tartu

BLUE HUMANITIES

Storied Waterscapes in the Anthropocene

Serpil Oppermann
Cappadocia University

CAMBRIDGE
UNIVERSITY PRESS

CAMBRIDGE
UNIVERSITY PRESS

Shaftesbury Road, Cambridge CB2 8EA, United Kingdom

One Liberty Plaza, 20th Floor, New York, NY 10006, USA

477 Williamstown Road, Port Melbourne, VIC 3207, Australia

314–321, 3rd Floor, Plot 3, Splendor Forum, Jasola District Centre, New Delhi – 110025, India

103 Penang Road, #05–06/07, Visioncrest Commercial, Singapore 238467

Cambridge University Press is part of Cambridge University Press & Assessment, a department of the University of Cambridge.

We share the University's mission to contribute to society through the pursuit of education, learning and research at the highest international levels of excellence.

www.cambridge.org
Information on this title: www.cambridge.org/9781009393270

DOI: 10.1017/9781009393300

First published 2023

A catalogue record for this publication is available from the British Library.

ISBN 978-1-009-39327-0 Paperback
ISSN 2632-3125 (online)
ISSN 2632-3117 (print)

Cambridge University Press & Assessment has no responsibility for the persistence or accuracy of URLs for external or third-party internet websites referred to in this publication and does not guarantee that any content on such websites is, or will remain, accurate or appropriate.

Blue Humanities

Storied Waterscapes in the Anthropocene

Elements in Environmental Humanities

DOI: 10.1017/9781009393300
First published online: July 2023

Serpil Oppermann
Cappadocia University
Author for correspondence: Serpil Oppermann, serpil.oppermann@gmail.com

Abstract: By drawing on oceanography (marine sciences) and limnology (freshwater sciences), social sciences, and the environmental humanities, the field of the blue humanities critically examines the planet's troubled seas and distressed freshwaters from various sociocultural, literary, historical, aesthetic, ethical, and theoretical perspectives. Since all waterscapes in the Anthropocene are overexploited and endangered sites, the field calls for transdisciplinary cooperation and encourages thinking with water and thinking together beyond the conventions of tentacular anthropocentric thought. Working across many disciplines, the blue humanities, then, challenges the cultural primacy of standard sea and freshwater narratives and promotes disanthropocentric discourses about water ecologies. Engaging with the most pressing water problems, this Element contributes to those new discursive practices from a material ecocritical perspective. The author's hypothesis is that fluid-storied matter and the new stories we tell can change the game by changing our mindset.

Keywords: thinking with water, oceanography, limnology, wet matter, Anthropocene seas, Anthropocene blues, fluid-storied matter, aquatic agencies, freshwaters

ISBNs: 9781009393270 (PB), 9781009393300 (OC)
ISSNs: 2632-3125 (online), 2632-3117 (print)

Contents

Introduction

The true eye of the earth is water
Gaston Bachelard, *Water, and Dreams*

(1942/2006, 31)

We speak of geological time as if rock were the epitome of durability. It isn't.
Where rock meets water, it is water that wins in time, every time . . .
Amy-Jane Beer, *The Flow*

(2022, 59)

As a truly transdisciplinary field, the blue humanities studies planetary waters from sociocultural, literary, historical, aesthetic, ethical, and multiple other perspectives, and lays bare the broader social implications of hydrologic sciences.[1] The scholars in the field methodologically engage with the multivalent meanings of salt and freshwaters and the compounded changes all waterscapes are undergoing. The world's oceans, seas, lakes, ponds, rivers, streams, creeks, glaciers, and wetlands (i.e., marshes, swamps, fens, bogs, peatlands, estuaries, and bogs) are all in crisis today, brought about by capitalist regimes of power inhabiting the material-discursive spaces now traversed by the blue humanities. Blue humanities scholars entertain the propositions that the main problems and insecurities in aquatic ecosystems are ineluctably social and cultural; that the political systems mired within the capitalist logic are responsible for the damage inflicted on the planet's major waterways; and that the possibilities for any hopeful change are socially and culturally situated. Since our perceptions and ideas of water bodies are culturally shaped, as many scholars affirm, the best way to change the way people behave is to change the way they think. Thus, the field provides in-depth analyses of human relations with fluid sites from both material-discursive and sociocultural perspectives and offers analytical frameworks and critical pathways for studying these relations.

Accordingly, the task of this Element is to discuss human–aquatic interactions, including conceptual and metaphorical analogies of wet and dry worlds, as well as about water itself, on the one hand, and related scientific epistemologies of hydrosystems, on the other, as interactively explored in the field. I also deliberate on the discourses of narrative representations of waterscapes to signal the ideological nature of representation in narrative models. My discussion is modeled on the confluence of what came to be known as "thinking with water"[2] and the theoretical perspective of material ecocriticism.

---

[1] Hydrologic sciences are the fields of study concerned with Earth's waters (see footnotes 4,10, 11).
[2] The inspiration comes from *Thinking with Water* (2013) edited by Cecilia Chen, Janine MacLeod, and Astrida Neimanis.

The emergence of the term "blue humanities" is attributed to Steve Mentz who, in his 2009 article "Toward a Blue Cultural Studies," suggested that "some new developments in maritime studies" must be called "blue cultural studies" (2009a, 997). Four years later, ocean historian John R. Gillis published a feature article in *Humanities* titled "Blue Humanities" (2013), outlining the field's temporal development. In Gillis's preliminary outline, "[t]he emergence of the blue humanities is a belated recognition of the close relationship between modern western culture and the sea." However, the name of the field and the use of the term is not so new. Although not known among blue humanities scholars at the time, the term was first used in the 1940s by a famed Turkish author, Cevat Şakir Kabaağaçlı, who called himself the Fisherman of Halicarnassus and coined the term Blue Anatolian Humanism. British journalist Roger Williams explains in *The Fisherman of Halicarnassus* (2013) that the term refers to "the philosophy that developed during days and nights of discussion among the Fisherman and his Blue-ist (*Maviciler*) friends on their voyages along the Carian and Lycian shores" (2013, 92). Combining "classical literature with nature" (2013, 14), Blue Anatolian Humanism emerged from the conversations between the Fisherman and his famous intellectual friends during their Blue Voyages, which they initiated in Bodrum. Bodrum is the modern name for the ancient town of Halicarnassus, located at the junction of the Aegean and the Mediterranean seas, and where the author was exiled in 1925. Dating back to Ionians and Aeolians, the cultural heritage and the flora and fauna of Bodrum fascinated the Fisherman, inspiring him to write eleven story collections, five novels, eleven books of essays, and several memoirs, in many of which he claimed that this is where European civilization emerged. This "was the essential tenet of Blue Anatolian Humanism" (Williams 2013, 92), as evidenced in his prologue to his essay collection *A Flower Left to the Aegean Sea* (1972): "*This deep blue sky of southern Anatolia, its violet sea, light, and land, has nourished various trees, fruits, flowers, human beings, and civilizations*" (italics in the original).[3]

Other names have also been coined for the blue humanities, such as "new thalassology"[4] (Horden and Purcell 2006), "terraqueous ecocriticism" (Brayton 2012), "critical ocean studies" (DeLoughrey 2017), "humanist oceanic studies" (Price 2017), "hydro-criticism" (Winkiel 2019), and "blue ecocriticism" (Dobrin 2021). Since the oceans and their changing conditions were the prime targets of research in the field's developmental phase, they were extensively studied as sites of symbolic crossings and material connections among cultures, histories, and ecologies. That is why the field is commonly characterized by the

---

[3] For a more detailed account of the Fisherman of Halicarnassus, see my article "Enchanted by Akdeniz: The Fisherman of Halicarnassus's Narratives of the Mediterranean" (Opperman 2013).

[4] In ancient Greek Thalassa means "sea."

"oceanic turn" (Mentz 2009b, 2020; DeLoughrey 2017; Mentz and Rojas 2017; Winkiel 2019; Dobrin 2021), whereby scholars combine data provided by marine sciences with cultural and literary theories to modify our anthropocentrically oriented conceptions and discourses of planetary oceans. What is of utmost importance here is subverting the dominant assumptions about the seas as exploitable resources separate from the human sphere, thus emphasizing the coextensivity of human realms and the seas. Although "it cannot be our home," as Steve Mentz points out, the sea has always been part of human cultural reality "because of its metaphorical vastness," especially for "literary culture on a global scale" (Mentz 2022, 4). This coextensivity of aquatic naturecultures is not only metaphorical, however. As the Fisherman of Halicarnassus emphatically reminded his readers, it is also essential to life as we are all mostly made of water: "The bodies of land creatures are mainly composed of water. Human blood is salty like sea water" (Kabaağaçlı 1961, 246). Water in human bodies, as cultural anthropologist Veronica Strang explains, is mostly "'intra-cellular' – inside our cells. The other third is comprised of 'extra-cellular' fluids such as blood plasma, and 'transcellular' fluids, which surround the cells, carry nutrition and oxygen to them and remove metabolic wastes" (2015, 31). Mentz, too, draws attention to the interrelations of bodies, water, histories, and narratives: "multiple forms of water shape human bodies, and human histories. Different narratives become legible through our depictions of liquid salt and freshwater, gaseous vapor, and solid ice" (2022, 7).

In the blue humanities, the sea is envisioned both as a geopolitical agency and as a symbolic domain marked by the intersecting stories of the Anthropocene seas, social practices, and cultural forces. Initially, the sea narratives were mostly drawn from customary western discursive maps that usually harbor a colonialist mindset (especially the nineteenth century Anglophone maritime stories), but over the years the blue humanities has become more attentive to knowledges and narratives of non-western water cultures, thus enabling the configuration of a more capacious understanding of the role of global capitalism behind the decline of oceanic and/or hydrological systems.[5] Expanding its knowledge practices about what geographers Philip Steinberg and Kimberley Peters (2015) have termed "wet matter," blue humanities scholarship aims to raise critical awareness about the ongoing biophysical transformations in both salt and freshwaters, even if the field still maintains "a distinctly saline focus to date" (Campbell and Paye 2020, 1).

---

[5] Hydrology is the scientific study of the chemical and physical properties of Earth's waters and the interrelationship between water and the land surface. It is mainly concerned with the hydrologic cycle, such as groundwater, runoff, and precipitation. Hydrologic sciences are comprised of oceanography and limnology (see footnotes 10, 11).

In this Element, I attempt to balance this saline focus with a conceptual plunge into the overlapping salt and freshwater ecologies and discourses, and to read water as a fluid site of narrativity where diverse aqueous life-forms call for our attentiveness to their stories that run alongside human narratives, transmitting frustrating messages of ecological despoliation. There is no doubt that the life rhythms, biopsychical linkages, recursive cycles, and intricate interactions of aquatic multispecies are relentlessly disrupted, and that life in water can no longer exceed systems of domination that are primarily western in origin. What propels this massive disruption are the mastering visions that shape the collective social memory and cultural imaginaries of the world's waterscapes. Therefore, the extensive damage from human activities to the chemistry of the Earth's hydrosphere entails alternative modes of thinking about life that "extends far deeper into the Earth's subsurface," which "comprises a large proportion of the biomass on Earth" (Reith 2011, 287). Recent oceanic studies, for instance, indicate that the number of "described marine species vary from 150,000 to 274,000, and of those that may exist from 300,000 to over 10 million" (Appeltans et al., 2012, 2191). In addition, marine scientists have discovered that "the deep sub-seafloor harbors phylogenetically highly diverse communities of Bacteria and Archaea" (Reith 2011, 288). Once thrown off balance, the metabolic diversity in the deep seafloor might diminish with yet unknown consequences to life in general. Similarly, freshwater ecosystems, which constitute only 1 percent of the Earth's surface, are alarmingly destabilized, and the number of different species that cannot adapt to quickly changing conditions decreases, eliminating biodiversity.

The blue humanities has, therefore, induced new ways of interacting and thinking with water, and different narrative strategies to represent the contemporary urgencies about human–water relations. These relations comprise the story of intersecting biological, geological, chemical, climatic, economic, and sociopolitical forces, all irremediably enmeshed in the complexities of the Anthropocene,[6] which is "graphically evident in the case of the global ocean" (Chaturvedi 2022,164).

---

[6] Proposed by Paul Crutzen and Eugene Stoermer in 2000, the Anthropocene defines a "new geological epoch on the grounds that, for numerous environmental parameters, our planet has already far exceeded the natural variability of the Holocene Epoch" (Head, et al. 2022, 1). In 2016, the Anthropocene Working Group (AWG) of the International Union of Geologic Sciences (IUGS) voted to recommend the Anthropocene as a formal geologic epoch at the 35th International Geological Congress. On May 21, 2019, the AWG voted again, this time to designate the Anthropocene as a new geologic epoch. See the results of the biding vote by AWG, released on May 21, 2019, at http://quaternary.stratigraphy.org/working-groups/anthropocene/

1 The Blue Humanities: Crisscrossing Boundaries

Water reworks boundaries as much as it bounds; it territorializes as it deterritorializes.

Lowell Duckert (2017, 55)

Since the Anthropocene marks a seismic rupture in the Earth's hydrosphere as much as in its atmosphere, biosphere, geosphere, and/or lithosphere,[7] aqueous life is severely affected on many levels, and often irreparably so. The distressing stories of the bluefin tuna disappearing from the waters of the Bosphorus[8] along with marlins, lobsters, and mackerel, and, more recently, the massive mucilage outbreak in the Sea of Marmara, which lasted from fall 2020 until the summer of 2021, are some selected examples from Turkey to evince this rupture in the seas.

In the maritime Anthropocene, the "destructive exploitation of ocean resources" (Hau'ofa 2008, 49) creates such enormous tides of devastation that their story takes a more central position than similar stories besieging fresh-water ecosystems. That is why the blue humanities still prioritizes the imperiled seascapes, calling attention to Anthropocene-related issues in all oceanic systems, collectively called the World Ocean. Ocean warming, acidification, deoxygenation, deep-sea mining,[9] oil spills, overfishing, surface runoff, disposal of toxic waste, and thus the presence of pharmaceuticals, plasticizers, pesticides, and detergents in waters that cause endocrine disruptions in fish, all threaten marine ecosystems and aqueous life, from plankton and coral reefs to whales. These issues require a transdisciplinary engagement with the oceans and a "method of thinking with, engaging, and submerging into the ontological, material, political, and cultural body of the largest part of our biosphere" (DeLoughrey 2023, 146). Such a method necessitates crisscrossing the boundaries between marine and social sciences and the humanities with cultural and literary theories and water-themed artistic projects. Social sciences, and the humanities in particular, "provide us with a diverse range of tools, approaches, and methodologies through which we can come to better understand the multiple dimensions of human relationships with the watery part of our world"

---

[7] The litosphere is the outermost layer of the Earth, which is the crust of the Earth. Geosphere is a layer made of rocky material.

[8] The Bosphorus is Istanbul's strait that connects the Black Sea with the Marmara Sea, separating Europe from the Anatolian peninsula.

[9] Deep-sea mining is the extraction of mineral deposits from the deep sea (below 200 meters), such as manganese, silver, lithium, nickel, cobalt, zinc, and copper, which harms deep marine life, and damages hydrothermal vents that contain sulfide deposits. Since seabed mining is recognized to be harmful to vulnerable marine ecosystems, the International Seabed Authority (ISA) has developed rules for commercial mining and has issued twenty-seven contracts for mineral exploration, encompassing a combined area of more than 1.4 million km^2 (see Miller, et al. 2018). But despite the rules for commercial mining, extractive economies for mineral resources, such as manganese, are still in demand.

(McKinley 2023, xxii). The blue humanities has specifically enhanced our understanding of these dimensions by bringing attention to new art practices that highlight the fragility of oceanic habitats. As art curator Stephanie Hessler has also pointed out, taking an aquatic turn, contemporary art provides "methodologies that are hybrid, transdisciplinary, generative, fluid, uncertain and transformative" and involves "various forms of knowledge, both human and nonhuman" (2020, 250). In this approach, art, culture, and literature not only propound new cognitive modes of connecting with the seas but also help bridge the biocultural separation between the land and the sea, situating our thinking within the crises-ridden and traumatized Anthropocene seas. Since the Anthropocene "affects conceptual frameworks as much as material realities" (Hessler 2020, 256) of the seascapes, it necessarily instigates transdisciplinary studies of the world's expansive salt waters.

Enabling a shift "away from dominant narratives of state conquest and technological mastery" (Anderson et al., 4), transdisciplinary scholarship in the blue humanities problematizes the traditional conceptualizations of the seas as spaces for aesthetic and spiritual contemplation, or as unpredictable, formidable enemies that need to be subjugated. To subvert this binary thought, and to "balance the oppositional forces of lure and dependence, alterity and need" (Mentz 2021, 186), the field espouses a transformation of anthropocentric discursive practices regrettably entangled in what Serenella Iovino calls "bioschizophrenic modernity" (2021, 4) through recourse to the scientific knowledge of the World Ocean's biogeochemical cycles and biosystems in naturalcultural practices. Another important characteristic of the field is that, although "it has unfolded predominantly within the scholarly communities of the Anglophone West," as emphasized by Søren Frank, "recently, there is increasing interest in the maritime global south, including the Indian and Pacific Oceans and their roles in the societal history of the East" (2022, 12). With this interest, there has been significant resistance to the previously unquestioned ideology of western discourses by which the seas are represented in arts and literature. Based on Eurocentric modes of representation, the traditional narrative models (historical and fictional) were shown to be rather inadequate for the task of narrating the World Ocean as they are – sometimes inadvertently, sometimes purposely – complicit in capitalist notions of property and ownership (Gilroy 1993; Steinberg 2001; Bélanger 2014; Bystrom and Hofmeyr 2017; DeLoughrey 2019a; Perez 2020). There is, in fact, a long and rather anthropocentrically oriented tradition of the interaction of literature (both western and global) and seascapes with innumerable canonical texts, and that "Western literary history (as well as global literatures) is awash with representations of ocean" (Dobrin 2021, 15). As Margaret Cohen famously wrote: "At the dawn of Western narrative, Homer's Odysseus sets sail" (2010a, 1), and storytellers since the time of Homer have been immersed in a shared mode of figurative representation. Those representations, however, were either disconcertingly colonialist or resolutely romantic, but at the same time they presented a liberating challenge to review the major indexes of conventional sea discourse: literary, historical, cultural, and political. Joseph Conrad's narrative of the Indian Ocean in *The Nigger of the "Narcissus,"* Herman Melville's descriptions of whale hunting in *Moby Dick*, Samuel Taylor Coleridge's romantic discourse in *Rime of the Ancient Mariner*, and Ernest Hemingway's narrative of the epic struggle between a marlin and an old fisherman and later between sharks and the fisherman in *The Old Man and the Sea* are only four exemplary canonical British and American maritime narratives that depict the ocean as awe-inspiring and uncontrollable. This so-called binary view of the ocean, Elizabeth DeLoughrey concurs, is "a long western tradition," as these narratives represent the ocean in terms of "the sublime that is simultaneously 'mystery' as well as a site for conquest" (2023, 151). This is evident, for example, in Joseph Conrad's reckoning of the sea. In his 1898 essay "Tales of the Sea," Conrad writes that for him the sea was "a stage, where was displayed an exhibition of valour, and of achievement the world had never seen before" (qtd. in Carabine 1998, ix). For Conrad, "[e]verything can be found at sea … strife, peace, romance … ideals, boredom, disgust, inspiration" (Carabine 1998, ix).

Inspired by the new discoveries at the time and seafarers' adventures, the themes of such narratives were bravery and heroism that trumpeted in the language and mentality of conquest; therefore, they are "often cataloged as nautical fiction, naval fiction, or maritime fiction, categories that intimate connections to military valor, colonial exploration and conquest, and nationalism" (Dobrin 2021, 21). This is first examined by Margaret Cohen in her seminal book *The Novel and the Sea* (2010), which is a comprehensive literary exploration of the western maritime world in the novel genre from the early modern period to the early 1900s. Cohen correlates the emergence of the novel with transatlantic history and interprets early British, American, and French novels in terms of maritime adventures and overseas explorations. Cohen's book is thus a detailed analysis of the sea as history and materiality. She also argues, in her article "Literary Studies on the Terraqueous Globe," that the "maritime world" emerges both as "a frontier of science and technology" and as "a great reservoir of books, narratives, and fantasy" (2010b, 657). But since those narratives were entirely masculinist, Sid Dobrin's description of them as "masculine conquest narratives" (Dobrin 2021, 16) is more realistic as they generated a literary tradition steeped in colonialist ideology and imperialist politics deemed to be necessary for western economic progress. To unsettle those narratives, the blue humanities has persistently encouraged new stories that would immerse us in speculative attention to aquatic life to cultivate better imaginative relations to the seas and to revise our ways of thinking and acting in the face of the devastating changes occurring in salt waters. What consequently dissolves in this revision are our anthropocentric shells that are the inevitable byproducts of globalized liberal-humanist cultures that regulate collective structures, minds, and social practices of world citizens.

My argument in this Element is that the blue humanities contests the assumptions of this kind of cultural inclination through new representational and discursive practices by promoting hybrid forms and strategies to confront the complex contemporary realities of seascapes. One of the best examples of such alternative art forms is the "Crochet Coral Reef" project: an artwork responding to the dying coral reefs, defined as "a nexus of art, science, mathematics, environmentalism, and community practice."[10] Another concrete example of hybrid strategies is a project called "Territorial Agency: Oceans in Transformation" (2020), commissioned by TBA21–Academy,[11] which brings together science, art, and culture to demonstrate that concerns about the oceans are simultaneously scientific, ethical, social, cultural, and artistic:

> Assessing the latest scientific knowledge about the effects of a wide array of human-induced interferences on marine and coastal ecosystems, the project reiterates the critical role of the oceans in respect to planetary survival. TBA21–Academy and Territorial Agency have collaborated with a network of researchers and institutions to give exposure to new forms of visibility and understanding the ocean brought by science, culture and art. (2020)

Overall, emerging from the overlap of theory and marine sciences with aesthetic expressions, these refigurations foreground our world's changing ontology and the ways in which human–sea relations unfold in these transformative times. In such projects, the scientific data provided by oceanography, marine biology, and deep-sea ecology[12] become integral to understanding the biophysical properties of seascapes and their terraqueous connectedness. Often, scientific particulars are

---

[10] See https://crochetcoralreef.org/about/theproject/.

[11] Established in 2011, TBA21–Academy's research center promotes "a deeper relationship to the Ocean through the lens of art to inspire care and action. The Academy has been an incubator for collaborative research, artistic production, and new forms of knowledge by combining art and science for more than a decade" (www.tba21.org/#item%2Cacademy%2C1819). The quotation is from the 2020 Exhibition *Territorial Agency: Oceans in Transformation*: www.ocean-space.org/exhibitions/territorial-agency-oceans-in-transformation.

[12] Oceanography is the study of the ocean and its physical and chemical properties, as well as the geology of ocean systems. Marine biology is the study of marine organisms in the oceans, from the microscopic picoplankton to sharks and whales. Deep-sea ecology studies seafloor ecosystems and deep-sea geosphere–biosphere interactions, which are important in engendering biodiversity in the oceans.

crucial in framing urgent issues and questions about water ecologies and human interactions with the aquatic world. But interpreting scientific data is not an isolable process; it raises a host of questions related to economic, cultural, social, political, and ethical, as well as literary and aesthetic, domains, which help provide a more integrated approach to oceanic ontologies. When theory and science overlap to produce a counterforce against the dominant ideological formations of these domains, we can expect a discursive transformation and, ultimately, a paradigm shift. It seems to me that a world-engaging theoretical practice mediating scientific information would be particularly relevant for more ecologically oriented modes of understanding waterscapes. In other words, if the contested ideas about wet matter (i.e., ideas immersed within power structures that produce material effects) change, then their long-running legacy can dissolve in the waters along with their implicit blueprints in human minds. And this is possible. Let me emphasize the point that blue humanities scholars challenge the old paradigms of water ecologies in a way similar to how feminist and postcolonial scholars and ecocritics who have subverted hegemonic discourses that foregrounded (overtly or covertly) sexism, racism, speciesism, militarism, extractivism, and, above all, anthropocentrism, all rooted in a defunct geopolitical order perpetuating our "chronically exploitative relationships" (Estok 2021, 438) with the more-than-human environments. To develop effective critiques of this order and the Anthropocene oceans, the blue humanities rests its arguments on such questions as: In what ways can new literary texts, cultural works, and artistic projects enable us to comprehend the oceanic tragedies in the face of the Anthropocene? How do these tragedies intersect with issues of environmental and social justice and ethics of relations? How can artistic figurations and new narratives of the seas help deconstruct the capitalist, neo-colonialist, and imperialistic practices?

1.1 Expanding the Field's Horizon

The questions posed here are also valid for freshwater ecosystems. As Steve Mentz notes with good reason, "[d]espite the overwhelming presence of oceanic literature and oceanic scholarship, not all the water that matters to humans floats in the World Ocean" (2021, 193). In another recent article, Mentz further claims that "[i]n moving beyond oceans, blue humanities scholarship follows an impulse that has long been present in oceanic writing" (2022, 3). This means that the field of the blue humanities is not merely critical ocean studies but a comprehensive field with a widening scope that includes the study of freshwater ecosystems and biomes, such as lakes, rivers, streams, glaciers, and other freshwater systems. With this expanded horizon, the blue humanities invites a relational aqueous ontology in which salt waters and freshwaters are seen as integral parts of all planetary water ecologies with their co-constitutive and dynamic relationalities. In other words, oceanography and limnology[13] are not categorically different; rather, they are confluent in their figural notions and fates about their commodification, inviting a closer investigation of their "naturalized aesthetic/cultural/fictional/historical appropriations" (Oppermann 2019, 446). This categorical similarity was suggested by John A. Downing, the most recent past president of the Association for the Sciences of Limnology and Oceanography (ASLO) in his 2014 plenary address to limnologists, titled "Limnology and Oceanography: Two Estranged Twins Reuniting by Global Change." Comparing marine systems and inland waters suffering from similar human-induced threats, Downing notes that inland water is a "strategic resource" and "is essential to life," and that "inland waters contain more species disproportionately with their spatial extent (i.e., ~15–25% those found in marine systems)" (2014, 216, 217). What is of interest here for the blue humanities is Downing's valid claim about limnology and oceanography being two estranged twins that are reunited by global climate change. According to Downing, "[a]lthough frequently thought of separately, these disciplines share much history, many converging research paradigms, and, I believe, a common future" (2014, 217). Downing emphasizes especially "the urgency of the joint mission of limnology and oceanography toward sustaining a healthy interface between marine and freshwater" (2014, 215). This joint mission is highly significant for the blue humanities. Since both salt and freshwater habitats are imperiled sites equally exposed to human "fantasies of conquest and consumption" (Bennett 2010, ix), thus encountering similar hazards and issuing similar distress signals, the blue humanities can be both oceanic and limnological with its transdisciplinary focus on all aquatic systems, while studying them from literary, aesthetic, social, and cultural perspectives.

What emerges from this confluence of oceanography, limnology, and literary and cultural studies is a navigable "fluid poetics" (Jue and Ruiz 2021, 2), which makes the field undeniably "characterized by disciplinary fluidity" (Bakker 2019). Since all water environments are ontologically fluid sites, fluid poetics is the right mode of reflecting on and representing the conceptual, sociocultural, and ecological

---

[13] Limnology is the scientific study of freshwaters and is a subsystem of hydrology, which is the science that studies the distribution, movement, and properties of all waters and their relationship with the environment (see Wetzel 2001). Traditionally, limnology studies inland bodies of water, including lakes, ponds, rivers, springs, streams, and wetlands. One important aspect of limnology "is the synthetic integration of geological, chemical, physical, and biological interactions that define aquatic systems" (Dodds and Whiles 2010, 2).

challenges salt and freshwaters are facing today. Ultimately, aquatic problems are not only ecological; they also carry ethical and sociocultural imperatives, all of which are significantly shaped by discursive formations imbued with anthropocentric ideologies. Focusing on the physical complexities of water and its "imaginative polyphony" (Mentz 2021, 93), the blue humanities challenges those discourses that have infused our thinking and acting and thus valorized all strategies of domination. Hence, what flows beneath the lithic stories of the Anthropocene in the liquid habitats is exceedingly dark and demoralizing, with the ongoing exploitation of all waterscapes. If the world's hydrocommons are seriously disenchanted today – like rivers that suffer a worse fate than T. S. Eliot's "river" in *The Wasteland* that "sweat[ed] oil and tar" exactly 100 years ago (1930/1958, 39) – we need a more cohesive ecological approach to freshwaters as well, which constitute about 3 percent of all waters on Earth, compared to the oceans and seas that cover 71 percent of the Earth's surface. In this regard, the field's expanded focus on the sources of our exploitative relationships with both salt and freshwater ecologies reveal what Diana Coole and Samantha Frost would have said if we just replace "nature" with "waters" in their memorable line: "the ways we understand and interact with *waters* are in need of commensurate updating" (2010, 5). This updating is in progress today with the conjunction of sociocultural, literary, historical, ethical, political, and aesthetic discourses of the world's oceans and freshwater bodies with those of marine and freshwater sciences, all of which provide a viable onto-epistemological framework for rethinking the relations between waterscapes and landscapes, and between terrestrial humans and aquatic nonhumans. Reckoned with new theories and narratives from the arts and the humanities, the field constructively uses scientific data provided by marine sciences and now by the "recent hydrocultural research" (Campbell and Paye 2020, 1) on freshwaters.

Such a comprehensive horizon constitutes the field's identity in a relationship of constant slippage between the geophysical properties and discursive constructions of waterscapes. Having this "twofold condition," as I have previously underlined, the sea, in particular, is both "a physical geographical site and a vast domain of imagination that can never be conclusively charted" (2019, 446). Or, as Donna Haraway would say, like land and everything else in this world, the sea is "simultaneously literal and figurative" (1997, 11), and freshwaters are not exempt from this characterization. Thus, with complementary use of stories from cultural, literary, anthropological, and scientific accounts, the field forges a new conceptual map for the composite reality of the changing waterscapes to "sensitise humanity as a whole to the implications of this knowledge," as British physicist Alan Cottey argues about such ecological emergencies (2022, 819).

Therefore, relevant critical theories and modes of analysis from cultural and literary studies, visual arts, and sciences have become indispensable tools in the quest for sustainable solutions to heavily traumatized oceans and freshwaters. To find less anthropocentric ways of thinking about the planet's waterscapes, the blue humanities raises "potent questions about scale, temporality, ontological inter-connection, materiality, and mediation within the aquatic Anthropocene" (Alaimo 2019, 431). As such, aquatic scholarship has prompted a radical shift in the conceptual models of waterscapes by dispensing with the human-centered figurations of water bodies and reconfiguring "water as that which both connects us and differentiates us, as that which we both are and which facilitates our becoming" (Neimanis 2017, 111). If water *both* connects and differentiates us, then we need to move beyond either/or interpretive categories and toward more comprehensive and inclusive methods of scholarship. This is already significantly underway in the field, with new, multiperspectival conceptual frameworks. These frameworks help modify anthropocentric epistemologies, instrumentalist ideolo-gies, and the dominant ontologies grounded in a fragmentary view of life, which create the habit of seeing reality in terms of separate fragments – hence the field's embracement of revisionary forms of knowledge that enable *thinking with* water and the construction of a new cognitive wet paradigm.

On the whole, the blue humanities undermines historically conditioned and ideologically determined notions of its represented subjects – troubled seas and distressed freshwaters – suggesting instead *thinking with* oceans, lakes, and rivers, which can mutually refashion our relationships with wet matter. Thinking with water means practicing "relational thinking, as theories based on notions of fluidity, viscosity, and porosity reveal" (Chen, MacLeod, and Neimanis 2013, 12), as well as recognizing seas, rivers, lakes, and all water bodies as living beings with innate rights. After all, water in every form has a right to flow unimpeded, and glaciers have a right to remain intact. The imperiled liveliness of waterscapes thus urges us to reimagine the collective story of conflicting and intimate terraqueous relationalities and to think through and across our contemporary situation against the present knowledge systems. Hence, as Andrew Biro maintains, "thinking with water today must not only maintain a sense of the real materiality of watery flows but also attend to the ways in which the structures imposed by thinking on those flows – 'basins,' 'watersheds,' 'aquifers,' 'oceans,' and so on – are abstractions, grounded in particular cultural understandings" (2013, 166–167). Such an outlook facilitates thinking beyond the disorienting framing of the Anthropocene, which "has come to signify a discourse embedded in the global scale vision of the sedi-mentary traces of the anthropos … instituting the human in the catastrophic knots of immutability" (Oppermann 2018, 2).

In a different register, then, this Element invites its readers to rise above this framing in a deeper understanding of aqueous life in the Anthropocene, which gathers us all, human and nonhuman, in planetary hydrocommons that are deeply interlaced with human mindscapes, reflexivity, and imagination. Significantly, these interlaced domains of waterscapes and mindscapes necessitate using what Astrida Neimanis calls an "onto-logic" to encourage us to think and act in a "logic of connection or communication" (2017, 94–95). Such an onto-logic not only entails thinking with water, but also helps us critically reflect on the symbolic meanings of the world's hydrosphere – meanings generated by traditional narratives that have played an influential role in determining our biocultural relations to water. To reform these relations, we need to let go of the old stories that cannot move us beyond the all too human frames. Because old stories, as Rebecca Solnit convincingly argues, "prevent us from seeing, or believing in, or acting on the possibilities for change ... Sometimes, the situation has changed but the stories haven't, and people follow the old versions, like outdated maps, into dead ends" (2023). To avoid being "hemmed in by stories" that lead us down blind alleys, Solnit suggests new stories. Australian novelist James Bradley (2017), too, offers a similar suggestion, advising us to find "new imaginative and lexical vocabularies capable of naming and describing concepts and experiences that exceed the human." The ecological constraints waterscapes face today have become so serious that it is clear how important new stories will be in the cultural imaginary if we want to have any positive change in our relations with the water worlds. I suggest that the new stories should reflect the cognitive vibrancy of the nonhuman in the storied waters, no matter how digressive or incoherent these narrative potentials may appear at first sight. Mainly, such stories can foreground the idea that, like solid matter, wet matter can be quite expressive, telling cautionary tales about the deteriorating water conditions and the slow demise of many species all caught up in the Anthropocene's rising waves.

If we accept the view that wet matter has an expressive agentic capacity with a signifying power ingrained in its aquatic entities whose meanings are deeply interlaced with human imagination via our literary traditions, then we come to realize that narrative, to borrow Roland Barthes's words, "is simply there, like life itself" (1977, 79). Storied water, in this regard, becomes the fluid ground on which the imaginary and the actual intersect in real and symbolic contexts. Reading storied waters "requires arts of imagination" (Swanson, Tsing, and Bubandt 2017, M8), as well as arts of attentiveness to recognize the expressive potentials of water itself and its narrative agencies. I offer this material ecocritical "poetics of water" (Mentz 2022) as a better alternative to the anthropocentric paradigm, which views eloquence only in human terms. This new interpretive horizon, which encourages us to be more perceptive of the stories and meanings of fluid matter, transforms our objectifying attitude to water-scapes and thus generates disanthropocentric modes of thinking.

This is a whole new approach by which we can, for example, read the oceans as if they continually transmit poignant stories of deoxygenation due to the flow of chemicals in the waters such as nitrogen and phosphorus, which produce harmful algal blooms with dangerous toxins. Ocean stories can also be read as an instance of what Rob Nixon calls "slow violence" (2011). The distressing stories of sea turtles that unwittingly eat plastic garbage thrown into the oceans and the stories of dying coral reefs are also instances of slow violence in the oceanic environments. Coral reefs[14] tell the saddest stories of being the most vulnerable victims of anthropogenic pressures; among them, ocean acidification and warming waters take center stage. Add to these flows of agricultural sediments, marine pollution, and overfishing to envision the darkening waves of the Anthropocene seas. In the specific case of corals, let us recall that they are made of calcium carbonate ($CaCO_3$) derived from seawater, and, when subjected to acidification in the water, their pH level is inevitably reduced. To raise the pH of the calcifying fluid, corals continue to produce calcium carbonate, but in acidic seawater they cannot bring carbonate ions to the level required for their skeletal growth. Moreover, the existence of coral reefs depends upon coral animals, such as polyps, which are anemone-like creatures that produce calcium carbonate crystals. By being stacked on top of one another, these animals form a skeleton to protect themselves. This enables coral reefs to survive in colonies in which skeletons of numerous polyps form domed structures, providing nesting grounds and food sources for many marine species, such as marine flatworms. Coral reefs also prevent beach erosion along tropical coastlines.[15]

The Status of Coral Reefs of the World 2020 Report plaintively reveals that although coral reefs occupy less than 1 percent of the ocean floor, they are home to more than 25 percent of marine life. The report also underlines the fact that coral reefs can recover when they are not disturbed by anthropogenic threats, and their story conveys a dynamic life under the ocean's surface where 800 different species of hard coral help marine life thrive. Because coral reefs harbor the highest biodiversity of any ecosystem, they are the most vibrant ecosystems now facing an existential crisis due to climate change and other human-induced stressors.[16] In "Scientists' Warning of an Imperiled Ocean," scientists reveal

[14] See the "Status of Coral Reefs of the World: 2020" report, produced by the Global Coral Reef Monitoring Network (GCRMN). www.unep.org/resources/status-coral-reefs-world-2020.

[15] This is my summary of the scientific information provided by Anne L. Cohen and Michael Holcomb (2009).

[16] See "Life Below Water," from the Global Coral Reef Monitoring Network of the International Coral Reef Initiative: www.unep.org/interactive/status-world-coral-reefs/.

how these stressors have accelerated damage to marine habitats, "with 76% of marine and estuarine species affected … including notable losses of 50% of coral-reef cover … and 40% of kelp forests" (Georgian, et al. 2022, 2). Being thus constrained by continuing stress, coral reefs project their stories through their dwindling colors as meaningful signs to convey their dying cries. Color is their primary tool of expression, used with mastery to stay alive and for conveying their sad stories. The decimation of the Great Barrier Reef in Queensland, Australia, is a striking example of such stories as it is the largest coral reef system in the world, with "400 types of coral, 1,500 species of fish and 4,000 types of mollusc." It is also the "habitat of species such as the dugong (sea cow) and the large green turtle, which are threatened with extinction."[17]

The stories of many species here make the Great Barrier Reef a major site of narrativity, whereby the reefs and their inhabitants "prompt us to rethink the scope of our deeds and attitudes" (van Dooren 2017, 63). Among the 1,625 species living in the Reef, the story of the iconic clownfish (seen in orange, white, and black), has become quite well known due to Disney Pixar's computer-animated film *Finding Nemo* (2003). Other species that live in the Great Barrier Reef include giant clams with psychedelic colors (the largest mollusc on Earth), manta rays, the colorful giant fish, the Māori wrasse, codfish that resembles a potato, dwarf minke whales, sharks, and turtles. Paying attention to the stories of these creatures, seeing them as expressive beings that communicate cautionary tales, is a material ecocritical vision that can expand our sense of awareness about their entangled fate with the overwhelming presence of human beings. These aquatic agencies, as Michel Serres would also affirm, can "speak just as much and perhaps better than us, they also say, write, sing, communicate among themselves, through a kind of reciprocal encoding, a kind of common language, a kind of music, harmonic, disharmonic – I don't know yet – but whose voices I am sure to hear" (2010, 131). Acknowledging their creative expressions is a good way to embrace more sea-friendly modes of thinking and acting.

Such an acknowledgment is well embodied in an artwork I mentioned earlier, the *Crochet Coral Reef* project, exemplifying the mingling of creative expressions in nature and culture in performative forms of creativity indicated by their interlacing threads. This innovative way of "crocheting a reef as a crafty response" to the plight of the Great Barrier Reef was inspired by the "unfolding of living ecologies where chance and circumstance are central drivers of innovation."[18] As is stated on the project's website, the artwork is "an artificial

---

[17] See UNESCO World Heritage Convention, "Great Barrier Reef" page: https://whc.unesco.org/en/list/154/.

[18] "The *Crochet Coral Reef* – a project by Australian twin sisters Christine Wertheim and Margaret Wertheim – is an artwork responding to climate change, an exercise in applied mathematics, and

ecology emerging from an exploration of *matter, form,* and *code.*" It is indeed
what Donna Haraway calls a "wooly experimental life-form." The other materials used, Haraway notes, are "[p]lastic bottle anemone trees with trash tendrils
and anemones made from *New York Times* blue plastic wrappers" (2016, 78). In
this fabulous habitat, we witness the unfolding of a "craft-based 'chemistry'
grounded in a language of the hands." This crochet artwork aims to produce
"lively looking seascapes, invocations of reefs . . . which act on a psychological
level to elicit in viewers a feeling of being 'down there' under the sea." What
makes this project so special is, first, how it shows the connectivity of human–
nonhuman creative expressions, and second, that it makes us aware of how
a "one-stitch-at-a-time meditation on the Anthropocene" can generate
a message of hope amidst the plight of the troubled seas.

2 Troubled Seas: Oceanic Imagination

We have seen that thinking *with* the troubled seascapes has given rise to an
oceanic turn in the humanities (DeLoughrey 2023), highlighting the crucial role
oceans play in shaping world cultures, literary narratives, aesthetic sensibilities,
artworks, economies, politics, moral codes, sciences, and even languages.
Many blue humanities scholars – including Elizabeth DeLoughrey, Steve
Mentz, Astrida Neimanis, Hester Blum, Laura Winkiel, Margaret Cohen,
Teresa Shewry, Rachel Price, Craig Santos Perez, Melody Jue, and Sidney
I. Dobrin, among others – have emphasized the material-discursive significance
of the oceans. Their work has moved the field "beyond the boundaries and
methodologies of land and nation-state-based environmental perspectives,
while also foregrounding the colonization, territorialization, and militarization
of the oceans" (Perez 2020, 2). To a large extent, then, the blue humanities has
come to be known as "Critical Ocean Studies" which, as Craig Santos Perez
rightly claims, "flows across disciplines; dives into submarine depths and
submersions; swims into multispecies entanglements; intersects with feminist,
indigenous, and diasporic epistemologies; recognizes the agency of a warming,
rising ocean; and transforms our critical inquiries and reading practices"
(2020, 2).

Flowing across disciplines, and referred to as the "oceanic turn" in academic
circles, critical ocean studies has indubitably enriched cultural and literary
studies as the sea is no longer considered to be an empty space to be claimed
by capitalism, a "passive setting for a dramatic narrative" (Slovic 2008, 6), or "a

---

a wooly experiment in evolutionary theory"; https://crochetcoralreef.org/artscience/overview/.
See also Margaret Wertheim (2015), Science+Art Project: Crochet Coral Reef: www
.margaretwertheim.com/crochet-coral-reef.

backdrop, a surface upon which humans, objects and ideas have travelled backward and forward" (Hofmeyr 2019, 2). Rather, the sea is now recognized as an active agentic force that has always been elemental to human life, and as a shaping presence of global cultural imaginary. In oceanic literary studies, sea-focused novels, with their rich figurative language, have won more favorable notice, but sea-themed poems, too, capture the symbolic expanses of the oceans and their multilayered material relations to human life – what I define as the sea's twofold condition. Perhaps, more intensely than novelists, poets, as Gaston Bachelard reminds us, "have felt the metaphoric richness of water contemplated in its reflections and in its depth *at the same time*" (1942/2006, 51, italics in the original). Poets have often intuited that the ocean, with its inherent dynamism, brings their creative potential to the surface, resulting in a more fluid poetic self that unfolds through the transformative impact of the poet's imaginative, material, and semiotic relation with the oceanic world. Moreover, the oceans relay a sense of how the fluid materiality of seascapes intersects with poetic imagination to create a deeper awareness of conflictual human–marine interactions and the sea's double modality, asking for what I call a "figurative submergence" (2019, 446) in its fluid materiality.

This double modality, as renowned postmodern author Raymond Federman once said, is marvelously "decoded into words" (1993, 89) in contemporary sea poetry in such a way that the troubled seas can both "sweet-talk" and gather the dark rhythms of the Anthropocene by tossing "havoc shoreward," as in Pulitzer Prize-winning poet Mary Oliver's poem "THE POET COMPARES HUMAN NATURE TO THE OCEAN FROM WHICH WE CAME" (caps original). This poem captures the sea's story of doubleness with expressive metaphors:

> The sea can do craziness, it can do smooth,
> it can lie down like silk breathing
> or toss havoc shoreward; it can give
> gifts or withhold all; it can rise, ebb, froth
> like an incoming frenzy of fountains, or it can
> sweet-talk entirely. As I can too,
> and so, no doubt, can you, and you. (2012, 65–66)

Although the sea's metaphorical richness emerges from its mysteries and has a captivating allure for poets, marine environments do not only carry metaphorical value; they are also physical agents, with the crucial role they "play in regulating the planet's climate" (Price 2017, 45). Their factuality and mystery are contemplated by Mary Oliver in her evocative poem "The Waves," which epitomizes this twofold ambiance of the sea, its dyadic profile as filled with mysteries as well as facts.

The sea

isn't a place

but a fact, and

a mystery (1986, 508)

Filled with facts and mysteries. That is indeed what the sea is all about. Though the poem never mentions facts such as tides or storms, its effectiveness lies in its simplicity to render its message – that the sea is a *fact*. The sea is also a *mystery*, which both storytellers and scientists consider "a curious story – but very revealing" (Zalasiewicz and Williams 2014, 35). The reason why the sea is a mystery goes back to the time of Homer, when people witnessed it to be full of unpredictable powers and signifying elements, which are reflected in countless stories across all cultures. That is, the sea is always compounded of textuality and materiality; it is both factual and metaphorical. In addition to this, the sea was and still is always/already storied as it can be interestingly expressive and creative, partaking in the collective poetry of life. Poets and novelists simply gave expression to this intuited truth. Take, for example, Salman Rushdie's fantastic character Haroun in *Haroun and the Sea of Stories*, who notices that the fish in the ocean are communicative and swallow "Story Streams." To his amazement, these fish always speak in unison with "perfectly synchronized words: 'Hurry! Hurry! Don't be late!' bubbled the first fish. 'Ocean's ailing! Cure can't wait!' the second went on" (1990, 84).

Another telling example is provided by Søren Frank in *A Poetic History of the Oceans* (2022), where he introduces and discusses in detail Danish writer Siri Ranva Hjelm Jacobsen's epistolary novel *Havbrevene* ([The Sea Letters] 2018). The novel, Frank explains, consists of letters exchanged between the Mediterranean Sea and the Atlantic Ocean (2022, 351). The Atlantic detests humans while the Mediterranean feels pity for them. Interestingly, Frank argues, "Jacobsen's choice of oceanic focalization provides the reader with nonhuman perspectives on planetary evolution and human history. Events in *Havbrevene* are geological, hydrological, and global in scale, but stories of human destinies and deeds are also told by the two oceans" (Frank 2022, 385). What becomes clear in Frank's exposition is that both the Atlantic Ocean and the Mediterranean Sea are enlivened as narrative agencies, telling stories of ominous warnings for human beings who either learn the ways of living in sustainable relations with the seas and all that exists within, or face extinction. It seems that the ocean and the sea represented in the novel perform an uncanny act beyond human control, forcing the human subjects to learn to cultivate sustainable connections with the marine habitats. Frank's interpretation demonstrates that literary stories help us under-stand the sea as a narrative agency – a signifying agency with creative expressions – that is eager to form a storied relationship with human subjects. Since humans have a basic drive for hearing stories, the stories aquatic agencies tell can change our social and cultural conditioning and our habits of seeing the wet reality in utilitarian terms, enabling us to conceive the world from the perspectives of aquatic nonhumans.

Let me offer one more striking example of the sea as a narrative agency, which appears in the opening of Morgan Llewelyn's novel *The Elementals* (1993). The sea speaks in a collective voice: "*Aswarm with life, we think trillions of versions of thought. Our sentience is in your blood, in everything that contains water. We are the sea.... We are watching. We are aware. We are the sea*" (n.p.; emphasis in original). The collective voice of the sea here invites a new understanding of its eloquence, evincing a clear instance of its narrative dimension by bringing attention to its nonhuman vitality through the sea's communal words, which of course serve the purpose of revealing the sea's creative surge to instill environmental awareness in the mind of its readers.

Being emblematic of aquatic eloquence, all these stories illuminate a path to awareness about "living oceans" (Zalasiewicz and Williams 2014,114), which can effectively transmit messages and stories that emerge through dynamic relations with humans themselves. Living seas, as shown in the aforementioned and numerous other literary texts, ask for finding common grounds for new understandings and complementary perspectives concerning their reality now undergoing momentous changes. To achieve a revised understanding of the maritime environments, let's heed Françoise Besson's words: "We simply have to listen to the world's rhythms, to pay more attention to what most of us regard as non-words, and thus maybe will we come to realize that the world has always expressed itself in an enchanting language guiding us onto the path to awareness" (2021, 80). The voices of the sea in the Anthropocene are not so enchanting because these voices – if we learn to listen well – are signaling warning messages about our deteriorating relations with the seascapes. This point is strikingly emphasized by academic-poet John Lane (professor of English and Environmental Studies) through his traveling geologist narrator in *Anthropocene Blues: Poems* (2017). The world's seas are troubled, and overly disenchanted by a "gnarly drama," which the geologist underlines in one of his poems, titled in capital letters: "WHILE SNORKELLING THE GEOLOGIST ENCOUNTERS E.O. WILSON AND HIS BOOK *THE SOCIAL CONQUEST OF EARTH*" (2017, 13). While snorkeling the geologist notices that the reef might be alive "though bleached much of its color / by our modern chemical toxins," and ironically calls himself "the planet's boss, / the big chief, the emperor of air, diesel fuel, / bow thrusters, and tax shelters." But, at the same time, gathering the Anthropocene's dark rhythms, the geologist "marvel[s] at reefs still carrying on like soldiers / in the great campaign of life" (2017, 13). With his geologist narrator who uses stratigraphic-poetic language, Lane expresses human guilt at being complicit in the losses of the Anthropocene (Cory 2019). Lane's *Anthropocene Blues: Poems* also troubles the narratives of maritime environments in the Anglophone literary culture that "originate[d] in early modernity and extend[ed] into the present" (Mentz and Rojas 2017, 4). For example, when Lane conjures up a colonial ship named *You're Screwed* in the same poem in which he says "the squid and parrot fish don't know" (2017, 13), he encourages his readers to think more critically about the "colony of ideas and images" (2017, 14) inscribed in the traumatic histories of all the seas colonized by western powers: the Pacific Ocean, the Caribbean Sea, and the Indian Ocean. Lane locates a similar trauma in the lives of the poor people in South Carolina in "THE GEOLOGIST SPEAKS OF PHOSPHATE" (2017, 39–40), which highlights "the extractive nature of capitalism as it affects the South Carolinian poor" (Genesy 2019, 248). As such, the geologist calls into question shameless human relations with the seas and wants us to feel the distress the Anthropocene seas are experiencing. Subjects of economic significance and capitalist control, the seas "continue to be radically instrumentalized: offshore zones territorialized by nation-states, high seas crisscrossed by shipping routes, estuaries metabolized by effluents … seabeds lined with submarines and plumbed for resources" (Bélanger 2014, 3), and aquatic species cruelly commercialized.

One of the most striking instances of thalassic distress is in the mournful story of the Sea of Marmara, which I briefly mentioned earlier. This is the story of the devastation caused by a mucilage outbreak in the sea. Mucilage is "a gelatinous organic material … that can reach great dimensions and cover large areas" (Topçu and Öztürk 2021, 270–271). Released by marine organisms under stress, these "exopolymeric compounds" (2021, 270), or sea snots ("deniz salyası" in Turkish), have impacted mainly the benthic species in the sea of Marmara. As Turkish marine biologists Nur Eda Topçu and Bayram Öztürk explain:

> Mucilaginous aggregates that end up deposited on the sea bottom may cause severe damage to benthic organisms by reducing light availability to algae and by suffocating sessile invertebrates including gorgonians … moreover, the degradation of this organic material may cause locally hypoxic and even anoxic conditions. (2021, 271)

In their coauthored article on the mucilage problem, marine scientist Başak Savun-Hekimoğlu and industrial engineer Cem Gazioğlu also write that as a nonsinking organic material in the upper sea, thus called sea snow, mucilage attracts bacteria and viruses and causes marine diseases (2021, 402). They list some of the enviromental conditions for mucilage: "i) the presence of excess nutrients (nitrogen and phosphorus), ii) high temperature, and iii) stagnant sea conditions" (2021, 405–406). The authors conclude that these conditions are mostly triggered by human-induced pressures, such as increased ship traffic, economic activities, industrial wastewater flows, overfishing, coastal destruction, and inefficient ecosystem management (2021, 410), all of which have had a negative impact on the Sea of Marmara. Though utterly traumatized by this recent mucilage outbreak, Marmara encountered even worse anthropogenic devastation in the 1950s, carved poignantly into our collective memory by Turkish novelist Yaşar Kemal in his much-referenced novel *Deniz Küstü* (1978), translated as *The Sea-Crossed Fisherman*. Kemal recounts "the massive slaughter of dolphins for their oil to be used in numerous industrial areas, which continued ... for a very long time till its ban in 1983" (Balcı 2021, 115). Underlining this "new industry in the production of oil from the dolphins" (Kıryaman 2019, 112), Kemal's tragic story – or his "heartbreaking narrative," in Adem Balcı's words (2021, 119) – presents an intended ruination of marine life in the Marmara Sea by unsatiable human greed, which resulted in a "wholesale massacre" of dolphins whose "cries ... still echo over the Marmara ... as they were caught-harpooned, dynamited or shot dead" (Kemal 1978/1990, 37). In the novel, the protagonist Fisher Selim cannot understand this mind-defying act of cruelty:

> Why all this killing, all this destruction? The human being is pliant, kind, sensitive, loving ... Then, why the anger, the rancour, the hate? Why when one is sated must a hundred thousand go hungry? And how can the one who is sated feel secure under all those watching angry eyes, how can he be so callous? (1978/1990, 35)

With such salient "literary waves" (Oruc 2022,148), the Marmara Sea – perhaps one of the early victims of the Anthropocene's ruthless aquatic progress – sends warning signals about its commodification by greedy economic systems and capitalism's narrow focus on material wealth at the expense of vulnerable marine life. Unfortunately, however, those signals have gone unnoticed, because today all the seas are "entering a new phase of largescale industrialization" (Allison, et al. 2020, 11), which alters their geophysical properties, including their salinity and acidity. This is also a phase of "[t]ransoceanic militarism – via sail, coal, steam, or nuclear-powered ships and submarines" (DeLoughrey 2019b, 23). And, bound to the interests of commercial establishments, the industrial accumulation that has reshaped marine ecosystems is not isolable from the accepted social systems and cultural mindlessness that valorize and justify the capitalist and/or colonialist ideologies behind this industrialization process. Ordinary people, institutions, bureaucracies, and even critics are inevitably implicated in such ideologies of domination, which are encoded in overlapping social and cultural discourses and enabled on the level of representation in fictional narratives. That is why we need to break away from the stories enmeshed in this logic of reference rendering the seas as expendable and re-envision them as geopolitical and geosocial entities with "active metabolic life" (Danovaro, Snelgrove, and Tyler 2014, 465). The active life in the sea was first brought to attention by Rachel Carson in the early 1950s. Carson wrote poetically about how sea plants, animals, plankton, and diatoms blossom and thrive in spring and how important it is to understand the language of the sea (1951/1961, 29–33). To exemplify, she reads the sediments in the seafloor composed by billions of shells, skeletons, and remains of minute creatures as an "epic poem of the earth," claiming that "we can read in them all of past history. For all is written here" (1951/1961, 72). My invocation of Carson is meant to disclose her intuitive sense of the sea as fluid-storied matter filled with meaningful expressions, which needed to be acknowledged here.

In this reframing, the seas and marine creatures emerge as narrative agencies capable of producing meaning through their "communicative relations" (Van Dexter 2022, 179), enabling us to "engage in collaborative storytelling activities" (Bencke and Bruhm 2022, 11), and prompt us to *think with* the storied seas. Even though we may partially understand the polysemous meanings confined within the expressive encounters of aquatic species, which may be beyond our human sensory perceptions, this new way of storying/reading the seas can elicit new metaphoric perceptions of thalassic reality. Metaphors play a strategic role in our narrative encounters with aquatic agencies simply because, as David Rothenberg reminds us, we cannot really avoid looking "into water as image and metaphor, listening to it as music, feeling it as rushing substance" (2002, xiii; xv). Hence the inevitability of metaphoric representations despite the disputes they have triggered in the field. But we need to use in our new stories what I call "living metaphors," which are part of the collective semiotic creativity of all life itself and can potentially direct our attention to the storied seas.

2.1 Fluid Metaphors

Given the fact that "water is the ultimate metaphor of fluidity" (Strang 2005, 105) and that innumerable cultural and literary narratives highlight "water imagination" and water's "metaphoric power" (Bachelard 1942/2006, 35, 52), blue humanities scholars particularly highlight how water imaginaries in the terraqueous Earth have shaped social and cultural meanings of water bodies, and how human interactions with waterscapes have impacted the fluid sites. Since water metaphors structure our ways of thinking about water, the blue humanities is right in insisting that we perceive "the world in watery terms" (Rothenberg 2002, xiii, xv). Metaphoric (or figural) representations are indispensable in configuring social imaginaries and cultural meanings of waterscapes and expressing and embedding water's ontological fluidity, mobility, and dynamism in cultural contexts. While these representations may render water habitats as protean and elusive, they also establish a symbolic relationship with water that may feel as real as any other relation. Symbolic relations themselves are forged in discursive conceptualizations, but that doesn't mean that wet matter is only a discursively constituted symbolic entity. Water's material reality, however, is not beyond the reach of meaning-making processes or discursive formulations, as water's meanings emerge through interpretive practices that are always entrenched in specific cultural, social, historical, and ideological discourses. Discourse here should not be equated with signifying systems outside material realities but as an integral part of the material phenomena – or, as distinctively formulated by Karen Barad, as "material-discursive practices" that are mutually constitutive and foreground "the relationship between discursive practices and material phenomena" (2007,146). Accordingly, metaphoric renderings of waterscapes are parts of the material systems that take their multiple and common meanings from the pools of entangled natural processes and cultural imaginaries. Water's multivalent meanings, then, emerge from both its metaphoric representations (in fiction, poetry, and arts) and its fluid materiality.

Blue humanities scholars, however, have critically argued that the discursive conceptualizations and metaphoric representations muddle and blur the material reality of marine environments (Blum 2010; Yaeger 2010; DeLoughrey 2017). Hester Blum famously declared "[t]he sea is not a metaphor," and claimed that metaphoric representations "render the sea 'immaterial'" (Blum 2010, 670). This is a misunderstanding of metaphoric meanings and/or the figural notions of the sea, because what we take to be a symbolic, figural, or metaphoric meaning is a way of relating in which the meaning is modulated in the interweaving field of the material and the discursive. This doesn't mean that metaphoric representations are an addition of something else to water's material reality; rather, when used disanthropocentrically, they effect a kind of a better cognitive response to the oceanic realities with a new focus today, dissolving anthropocentric foundations of figural representations. This is what the living metaphors will achieve as they will complicate any actual and imaginative participation in the anthropocentric traditions enshrined in the sociopolitical climate of the day. To give striking examples to living metaphors, let me quote the Fisherman of Halicarnassus again, who describes the Mediterranean fish as "the chief birth givers" of sea, and fish eggs as "tiny round blue lanterns in the vast darkness of the sea." When the fish "discharge eggs, milk, and a flood of offspring," the Fisherman writes, the sea "turns 'milky white'," which, he says, is "the reason why the Mediterranean is called The White Sea in Turkish" (1961, 243).

In what follows I draw on previous work (2019) in which I argue that behind the criticism of metaphors lies the conviction that metaphoric representations of the World Ocean "stimulate totalizing strategies of domination and exploitation" (447), instigate "a mastering vision to colonize its resources and inhabitants quite ruthlessly," and thus "inadvertently play a role in the construction of anthropocentric ideologies, and in expanding a particular hegemonic discourse" (449). The blue humanities seeks to subvert such contestatory narratives but cannot dismiss them altogether because, as Melody Jue reminds us, "[e]ven when we believe we are speaking literally," we cannot really escape the "subconscious uses of metaphor" (2020, 3, 7). And even in scientific accounts it is not easy to avoid metaphoric language, which provides a good frame of reference for scientific terms. As cognitive psychologists Dedre Gentner and Michael Jeziorski contend, "[an]alogy and metaphor are central to scientific thought. They figure in discovery, as in Rutherford's analogy of the solar system for the atom or Faraday's use of lines of magnetized iron filings to reason about electric fields" (1993, 447). A more recent example is from oceanographer Roger Hekinian, who calls hydrothermal geysers "black smokers" and describes them as "fountains or strong jets of mineral-laden water spewing from hydrothermal chimneys several meters tall" (2014, 147).

If metaphors are inescapable even in scientific statements, then they work well as cognitive devices to spread the knowledge gained through scientific research. The scientific data provided by oceanography, marine biology, and deep-sea ecology, then, become more relatable and accessible. In his Preface to the fourth *World Ocean Review* (2015) on "Sustainable Use of Our Oceans – Making Ideas Work," Nikolaus Gelpke succinctly explains this process of interpretation:

> Our scientific knowledge … has become more diverse and multifaceted, creating something of a barrier to understanding and making the lessons to be learned from science less accessible. This applies especially to our oceans. Over recent decades, we have learned, for example, that chemical, biological and physical processes in the marine environment influence each other and cannot be viewed in isolation, requiring a more integrated approach to our *interpretation of scientific data* and showing that there no simple answers to the multitude of questions arising in modern marine research. (italics mine).

Interpretations of scientific facts and statistics, therefore, spill over to the cultural sphere, affecting perceptual and ideological transformations and amendments in the production of hydrological knowledge. Transmitting this knowledge by way of new stories becomes particularly important in making the meanings of this world more comprehensible and giving "shape to our understandings about the world." (Bradley 2017). Colored with the sea's undeniable metaphorical potency and not channeling anthropocentric ideology, such stories would, foremost, highlight the expressive creativity of sea creatures by navigating through the imaginary and the worldly. They would also offer a frame of reference on the complexity of this watery world, encouraging us to rethink our interactions with oceanic realities. Moreover, narratives that employ living metaphors can capture the storied dimension of the living oceans by opening our minds to their material-semiotic intensities and thus transform the controlling and the exerting power of "our deeply ingrained habits of thought" (Stengers 2013, 176).

Stories of fluid matter emerge from biological and abiotic systems alike, and all material agencies (aquatic and telluric) produce "configurations of meaning and discourses that we can interpret as stories" (Iovino and Oppermann 2014, 7). The ocean in this vision is a storied subject with narrative trajectories created by its innumerable denizens. Even if some are quite alien to the human observer, they can express themselves with sounds, colors, gestures, and, for example, bioluminescence (such as the viperfish in the mesopelagic zone of the ocean known as the twilight zone),[19] thus engendering what I call a "hydro-material story" (2019, 460). Literary texts that replenish hydro-material stories can be seen as narrative explorations of how the storied seas can make the aquatic voices familiar to our cognition, revealing their signifying nature. The human–sea relations the literary texts represent figuratively (and sometimes even literally, as in Yaşar Kemal's plaintive narrative) epitomize hydro-material stories as they also emerge from the fluid ontology of the seas, binding us in what Joanna Zylinska terms a "liquid dynamic of exchanges" (2021, 46). I interpret this as exchanges between human and marine subjects that inspire entangled stories in which the sea is as much a lively, agentic subject as is the human counterpart. This was well known by the Fisherman of Halicarnassus, who conceived the Mediterranean and the Aegean seas as living entities which, he believed, deserve recognition; therefore, he dedicated his stories to them, "*to the violet seas,*" as well as to "*mountains, grass, coasts, wild rocks, ruins, and open seas*" (Kabaağaçlı 1972, Prologue, emphasis original). The Fisherman's approach in his entire oeuvre foregrounds not only the storied dimension of the seas but also the essential need for a new way of thinking about their vibrancy to disavow the anthropocentric paradigm, which has exacted a heavy toll on the

---

[19] Viperfishes possess photophores, a glandular organ with luminous spots, to glow and glimmer. Many other marine organisms, including algae, jellyfish, crustaceans, sea stars, fish, squids, and even sharks, have light-producing ability, which is a process known as bioluminescence. It is the most common form of communication on the planet. For detailed information, see https://ocean.si.edu/ocean-life/fish/bioluminescence.

World Ocean. The solution, the the Fisherman suggested, was to acknowledge the intrinsic relationality of all things, which is at the root of his Blue Anatolian Humanism. Grounded in the awareness of the copresence and the coextensivity of the natural and the cultural, the Fisherman's vision can be a useful reference point for contemporary blue humanities studies of the water worlds endowed with geopolitical and sociocultural meanings.

If we define the World Ocean in terms of "inhuman magnitudes and wholly alien phenomena" (Cohen and Foote 2021, 3) – certainly a very powerful metaphoric take – we can perhaps better understand why our capacity to respond is overly land-based, which distances us from the unfamiliar oceanic environments. Consider the terms "littoral," "pelagic," and "benthic,"[20] enough to create a mental barrier let alone physical distance. But we need a different distancing today, to estrange ourselves, our mental ways, and even our theories, from familiar territories, to defamiliarize our habits of worlding. In a way, we have to relearn to think with the oceans anew, to "think within and through them as embodied observers" (Jue 2020, 3). For Jue, this method "productively estranges the terrestrially inflected ways of theorizing and thinking to which we have become habituated" (2020, 6). Joanna Zylinska, too, proposes an ontological shift toward being and thinking with water, which is "underpinned by a multiple ethico-political demand: to repair historical injustice that has resulted in the impairing of our own 'Western' epistemological frameworks and to learn from others about how to think and live otherwise" (2021, 65).

Thinking with the oceans begins with recognizing the sea as a "living thing with a history, geography, and a life all its own" (Gillis 2013). Such a recognition, first and foremost, denatures our habit of envisioning the seas as "places for stealing resources, dumping trash, and making money through shipping, oil drilling, and so on" (Yaeger 2010, 5330), and motivates us to rethink our conceptualizations, our metaphors, and our figurative language, so that we can learn to listen to the voices of troubled oceans. In short, understanding the sea as a living agency can effectively help overthrow the foundational metaphors of anthropocentric language, and also help resist our own simplistic tendency to see the world in binary terms.

3 Troubled Seas: Scientific Accounts

Scientists regard the ocean as an important sink for CO_2, which has absorbed approximately 30 percent of anthropogenic carbon (inorganic carbon resulting from human emissions to the atmosphere) between the industrial revolution and

---

[20] The littoral zone is the closes part of the sea to the shore, mostly known as the coastal areas, but no sunlight can penetrate the pelagic or benthic zones of the oceans.

the mid-1990s (Gruber et al., 2019). According to the analysis from NOAA's Global Monitoring Lab, the global average atmospheric carbon dioxide was 414.72 parts per million ("ppm" for short) in 2021,[21] which is higher than anything seen in the past 3 million years. This excess CO_2 in the ocean not only changes seawater chemistry but also affects ocean circulation, the function of which is to regulate climate, weather, and sea levels, and to "redistribute heat, freshwater, carbon, and nutrients all around the globe" (Berx, et al., 2021, 10). Ocean acidification occurs

> through the absorption of atmospheric CO_2 with open-ocean surface pH declining by a range of 0.017–0.027 pH units per decade since the late 1980s, threatening the survival of particularly soluble organisms, such as aragonitic pteropods. Increasing acidity may raise the calcium carbonate compensation depth (CCD) in the deep ocean, causing the demise of carbonate-shelled deep-water benthic organisms. (Syvitski, et al. 2020, 4)

In simpler terms, when CO_2 dissolves in saltwater and decreases the water's pH value, it causes acidity, which in turn impacts marine organisms, from plants and bacteria to fish, and thus food webs, and, consequently, human populations.[22] With the increased "concentration of free H+ ions in the surface ocean" (Steffen et al., 2015, 1259855–6) that changes the surface water's carbon chemistry and thus the cycles of phosphorus and nitrogen, marine microorganisms, which play a central role "in the global carbon cycle as they function as a biological pump," can hardly sequester "anthropogenic carbon dioxide from the atmosphere in the deep ocean" (York 2018). Oceanographers have been observing these processes especially on phytoplankton (microalgae) in the upper part of the ocean as they require sunlight for their growth. Even though phytoplankton are equipped with "biochemical techniques for concentrating CO_2 inside their cells," and can tap "into the much larger seawater pool of dissolved inorganic carbon" (Doney, et al. 2015, 18), they cannot cope with increasing acidification. Thus, growing out of control, they produce toxins that can kill fish, shellfish, whales, dolphins, seals, and seabirds. It is stated in a recent study that as "drifters in seas and oceans," such planktonic organisms

> dominate life in terms of abundance and biomass … They are essential players in the functioning of marine ecosystems. Among them, microscopic algae called phytoplankton use sunlight to generate biomass from carbon dioxide and water, forming the basis of planktonic food webs, contributing about half of global primary productivity through photosynthesis, and producing about half of the world's oxygen. (Hablützel 2021, 20)

[21] NOAA 2022. "Climate Change: Atmospheric Carbon Dioxide"; www.climate.gov/news-features/understanding-climate/climate-change-atmospheric-carbon-dioxide.

[22] For further scientific information see the special issue of *Oceanography,* vol. 28, no. 2. June 2015.

All biochemical cycles that keep oceans alive are dependent on oxygen, the lack of which creates a condition called hypoxia. That is, if oxygen concentrations go below 2 milligrams per liter, then hypoxic conditions occur; for example, fish exposed to hypoxia are observed to experience reproductive impairment and sex changes. If this continues over long periods, the result is dead zones.[23]

When oceans become less oxygenated, warmer, and more acidic, they become corrosive, with consequent changes in the oceans' biochemistry and plankton organisms. Even though the chemistry of the oceans may change due to "biological processes (e.g., the growth of phytoplankton, respiration, and the process of making $CaCO_3$ bodies) and physical processes (e.g., changes in temperature and salinity, the air-sea exchange of CO_2)" (Shadwick, et al. 2021, 14–15), additional anthropogenic changes lessen the ability of the ocean to cope with increasing atmospheric CO_2. The 2018 *IPCC Special Report on Global Warming of 1.5°C* offers a detailed account of how "a wide range of marine organisms and ecosystems, as well as sectors such as aquaculture and fisheries" are affected (Masson-Delmotte, et al. 2018, 178).[24]

The warming of the oceans resulting in a dismaying acidification rate has also caused the unstoppable bleaching of coral reefs, which are projected to decline further in the years to come. Scientists observe that if the surface temperatures reach 2°C, 99 percent of coral reefs will bleach in the twenty-first century (Cheng et al., 2019, 251). Similarly, the 2018 IPPC report pointedly states that "the majority (70–90%) of warm water (tropical) coral reefs that exist today will disappear even if global warming is constrained to 1.5°C" (Masson-Delmotte, et al. 2018, 38). As this report underlines, the anthropogenic carbon dioxide the oceans have absorbed has led to unprecedented changes in their carbonate chemistry that were intact "for at least the last 65 million years" (Masson-Delmotte, et al 2018, 37). Other consequences of ocean warming include "melting sea ice and ice shelves directly through bottom heating … increasing marine heat waves … and altered impacts of natural variability" (Cheng et al., 2019, 251).

---

[23] When algae blooms decompose, they produce bacteria that consume all the oxygen in the water, creating anoxic (or dead) zones, where no marine life can flourish. Dead zones, then, emerge due to declines in oxygen levels of waters that can be both nearshore areas and open ocean regions. Scientists call this offshore and coastal hypoxia, which worsens with increasing acidity and global temperatures. See David Kidwell (2015) at the National Centers for Coastal Ocean Science website: https://coastalscience.noaa.gov/news/oceanic-continental-margin-dead-zones-emerge-threats-coastal-waters/.

[24] The full title is: IPCC, 2018: *Global Warming of 1.5°C. An IPCC Special Report on the Impacts of Global Warming of 1.5°C Above Pre-Industrial Levels and Related Global Greenhouse Gas Emission Pathways, in the Context of Strengthening the Global Response to the Threat of Climate Change, Sustainable Development, and Efforts to Eradicate Poverty.*

The subsequent 2022 report – IPCC Sixth Assessment Report on "Climate Change 2022: Impacts, Adaptation, and Vulnerability" – is even more alarming. The third chapter, "Oceans and Coastal Ecosystems and their Services," provides further details of the fundamental alterations in the chemical characteristics of the oceans, and in oceanic and coastal organisms – from microbes to mammals and individuals to ecosystems (2022, 3.3). The 2022 report specifically highlights the impacts of climate change on the biota of the oceans and biological processes in deep-sea ecosystems (2022, 3.96) by drawing attention to "the globally projected declines in total seafloor biomass of –9.8% and –13.0% by 2081–2100 relative to 1995–2014" (2022, 3.96). Oxygen loss affecting deep-sea biodiversity, the report states, "could pose a significant risk to associated ecosystems" (2022, 3.97). Climate-driven impacts, then, not only limit the resilience of deep-sea ecosystems but also diminish the adaptive capacity of marine ecosystems. Hence the changing biodiversity "in association with ocean warming and loss of sea ice" (2022, 3.104). The general health of marine life is further pressured by another human disturbance to the oceans – namely, introduced species: "Sometimes these were moved deliberately for aquaculture, as with shellfish, such as oysters. More often, they have been moved invisibly and unwittingly in the ballast tanks of ships" (Williams and Zalasiewicz 2022, 187).

Climate-related changes in the temperature of the oceans, changes in water's salinity levels, and shrinking glaciers[25] are exacerbated by aggressive human exploits and relentless trespassing on aquatic domains. The alarming threats to the marine ecosystems posed by, for instance, methane hydrate mining for subsea gas production, offshore oil production (i.e., the 2010 disaster at the Deepwater Horizon drilling rig in the Gulf of Mexico),[26] and industrial over-fishing already make the future unpredictable. Authorized by social systems of power, industrial fishing is inflicting enormous damage on fish populations, as clearly stated on the *Seaspiracy* (2021) documentary website: "Fishing has wiped out 90% of the world's largest fish." When industrial human activities increase, so does the warming of the oceans. But we should keep in mind that for as long as the oceans are regarded as profitable commodities, they will act back on us with worse physical consequences. This so-called boomerang effect in social psychology can be observed, for example, on the livelihoods of more than 3 billion people who depend on the already precarious life in marine ecosystems

---

[25] See Daniel Glick's article "The Big Thaw" (2019), which gives a detailed account of how thawing thermofrost has led to ground sinking.

[26] When BP's Deepwater Horizon drilling platform exploded on April 20, 2010, eleven workers were killed and seventeen others were badly injured. "Two hundred and ten million million gallons of crude oil leaked into the Gulf of Mexico, the second-largest oil spill ever and the largest in American history" (Pinnix 2022, 75).

undergoing chemical and biophysical transformations.[27] We also need to consider the biggest threat to the ocean's health and its life-forms, namely the innumerable amounts of plastics disposed of in the oceans, making us and aquatic beings so entrapped in "the emergent flows of chemical toxicity" that we don't have the luxury to "retreat into a statis" (Davis 2022, 83).

These are indeed troubling times for the World Ocean.

3.1 Oceanic Plastic

Nothing could be more disenchanting for the oceans than the super agency of infamous plastic (synthetic or semisynthetic organic polymers)[28] swirling in deplorable toxicity flows. It is perhaps the longest chapter in the exhaustive narratives of the oceans. The shocking revelation of this chapter in oceanography is that there is an estimated 150 million metric tons of plastic waste in the oceans, which accumulates as microplastic fibers "in marine sediments on a global scale" (Gabbott et al., 2020, 36). The Pacific Garbage Patch – a vortex of discarded plastic garbage within the North Pacific Gyre, larger than Texas – is not only an index of the Anthropocene seas but also a terrifying reminder of the plastic trauma the oceans are suffering from, leaving vulnerable marine species totally defenseless. With stolen life, marine creatures cannot redeem their dwindling environments and annex them again to the ocean's vibrancy, but they can give expression to what has remained largely unexpressed in the social unconscious: the gauntlet of plastic pollution in human hands.

There is no escape from plastic takeover, as Brian Lieu expresses in the opening lines of his striking poem "Plastic," included in Craig Santos Perez's lesson on "The Poetry of Plastic" (2015):

> It never goes away . . .
> It kills, but can't be killed . . .
> The albatross was full . . .
> What's stopping us from being full
> one day . . .?
> (We're already fool . . .)

---

[27] See UN Sustainable Development Goals: www.un.org/sustainabledevelopment/oceans/.

[28] The word plastic was derived from "Plastikos,' which means 'to mold," in Greek. Plastics always include carbon and hydrogen. In fossil fuels, compounds containing hydrogen and carbon (hydrocarbon) act as building blocks for long polymer molecules. These building blocks are known as monomers, and they link together to form long carbon chains called polymers. Plastics are divided into two types: thermoplastic and thermosetting. Thermoplastic plastics can be deformed easily upon heating and can be bent easily. Linear polymers and a combination of linear and cross-linked polymers come under thermoplastics. Examples are PVC, nylon, and polythene. Thermosetting plastics cannot be softened again by heating once they are molded. Heavily cross-linked polymers come under the category of thermosetting plastics. Industrial plastic is made from petrochemicals. See https://byjus.com/chemistry/plastics/.

Plastic "can't be killed" because it is nonbiodegradable, and it has aggressively colonized the seas, as proclaimed by science studies scholar Max Liboiron (2018), who sees plastic pollution as a ramifying form of colonization; it is even found in the Arctic region and in the Mariana Trench, which is the deepest part of the Pacific Ocean. Oceanic plastic is also detected in the epipelagic zone of the oceans where sperm whales live.[29] The story of a dead sperm whale, washed ashore in Indonesia in 2018, with thirteen pounds of plastic trash in its stomach indicates the tragic outcome of seascapes besieged by discarded plastic. Oceanic pollution is, thus, the most disturbing case of how "the global commons have become deeply anthropomorphized through the byproducts of human production" (DeLoughrey 2019a, 101). The distressing stories of sea turtles tangled in discarded fishing nets, seals impacted by rapid ice loss, seabirds troubled by plastic ingestion, and many species of fish that also consume microplastics for food are emblematic of the deadly allure of plastics dismantling life in the oceans. These stories are within the purview of journalists as well. For example, in her article "Swirling Seas of Plastic Trash" (2011), science journalist Amanda Rose Martinez provides a succinct account of oceanic garbage that threatens marine life:

> Plastic trash in the ocean and on beaches harms sea animals of every size, from microscopic organisms called phytoplankton to whales. Some eat the trash, thinking it's food. The animals' stomachs fill up with garbage, and if they can't poop it out, they die. Other animals get tangled in the trash and drown. This trash may even contain dangerous chemicals that are making their way into the seafood we eat.

The widely known story of the Laysan albatrosses on Midway Island on the Northwest Hawaiian Islands in the North Pacific Ocean is another reminder of the plastic threat, which Chris Jordan publicized in his documentary *Midway: Message from the Gyre* (2009), showing how the birds consume macro- and microplastics and die. What is worse, plastic pollution "extends ... out into the world, throughout biological and geological strata" (Davis 2022, 38). The Center for Biological Diversity calls oceanic plastic a global tragedy for all sea life (fish, seabirds, marine mammals) and has petitioned the US Environmental Protection Agency to regulate plastics: "We've sued companies that turn plastic into consumer goods to better control their runoff. We're challenging the permits needed to build those new ethane cracker plants and organizing grassroots resistance to stop them."[30] Such actions can at least offer some hope for the future.

---

[29] The epipelagic zone, which reaches from the sea surface down to approximately 200 meters (650 feet), is home to whales, dolphins, sharks, billfishes, tunas, and jellyfish.

[30] See "Oceanic Plastic Pollution" on the center's website: www.biologicaldiversity.org/cam paigns/oceanplastics/.

Among all the publicized cases, Kamilo Beach on the Big Island of Hawaii is, perhaps, the most famous example of plastic takeover as it is filled with countless plastic objects of various sizes: plastic tubes from Japan, plastic bottles from Asia and America, toothbrushes from around the world, plastic netting, fishing lines, Lego blocks, little pellets, and many other objects of all sizes, which can be deadly as they break down, releasing carcinogenic chemicals such as Bisphenol A (BPA), DEHP, styrene, and phthalates. Because of its proximity to the Great Pacific Patch, Kamilo Beach is so overrun with plastics that blogger Kaylee Lozano calls Kamilo a "plastic beach" in her Beach Blog (2020). Since plastic does not biodegrade but photodegrades, it becomes brittle and continues to break up into smaller pieces, which never decompose. As oceanographer Charles Moore, geologist Patricia Corcoran, and artist Kelly Jazvac explain in their 2014 article "An Anthropogenic Marker Horizon in the Future Rock Record":

> Combined with abysmal rates of recovery, a massive amount of plastic debris has accumulated in Earth's waterways and along shorelines . . . These plastics have been proven dangerous to marine organisms and seabirds through ingestion, entanglement, and disruption of feeding patterns . . . In addition, adsorption of persistent organic pollutants (POPs) onto plastics . . . enhances the potential for bioaccumulation from ingested microplastics into fish. The unknown effect on apex predators, such as humans, is a major concern. These POPs, such as polychlorinated biphenyls (PCBs), can cause serious health effects, as they have been shown to be endocrine-disrupting chemicals and carcinogens. (2014, 4)

This article was published after the authors' trip to Kamilo Beach in 2013 in search of a "multi-composite material made hard by agglutination of rock and molten plastic" (2014, 5), which they called "plastiglomerate." Since this substance was anthropogenically formed, the authors refer to it as "a distinct marker horizon of the informal Anthropocene epoch" (2014, 6). Anthropogenic plastic pollution is now so widespread that it is also observed in deep-sea environments. A shocking discovery comes from marine geologists Guangfa Zhong and Xiaotong Peng, who witnessed significant plastic litter in "a submarine canyon located in the northwestern South China Sea" (2021, 581). Through seven manned submersible dives in May 2018, Zhong and Peng have documented large piles of benthic litter in the deep canyon floor. They conclude that "canyons may be a staging point for plastics that will ultimately be delivered to the deep ocean basins, where they will interact with delicate ecosystems, highlighting the need for mitigation of plastic waste dispersal into the natural environment" (2021, 586).

At present, however, "studies of chemical and biological plastic degradation in deep seafloor sediments are almost entirely lacking" (Kane and Fildani 2021, 607).

Scientists claim that even if plastic pollution abruptly stopped, the remaining macro- and microplastics will continue to break down, and any attempt to extract them from the seafloor would be even more dangerous than leaving them there, because such an attempt would be "akin to the scale of devastation caused by deep-sea mining" (Kane and Fildani 2021, 608). Further shocking news was the discovery of plastics in human blood,[31] breast milk, and cow's milk, where microplastics bioaccumulate in the form of phthalates. So, how do we solve this problem when the Anthropocene oceans are overflowing with plastic debris accumulating at the bottom of the seas, on the surface of waters along shorelines, and even in our blood and in mothers' milk? Science journalist Amanda Rose Martinez (2011) proposes an ordinary solution, which can be achieved if consumers discard their trash only into garbage cans and use less plastic, especially avoiding plastic packaging. This solution would only work if the production of plastic is made nonprofitable by effective laws and their implementation, because without practice and application laws are simply statements on paper. As a matter of fact, we need social reforms to persuade people and policymakers to adopt more eco-friendly lifestyles and policies.

3.2 Other Oceanic Threats

Plastic pollution, however, is not the only detrimental human signature in the seas. Another harmful cause of oceanic depreciation is anthropogenic climate change. The IPCC 2019 "Special Report on the Ocean and the Cryosphere in a Changing Climate" underlines cascading risks of climate-driven changes (e.g., sea-level rise, carbon emissions, oxygen loss, changes in nutrient cycling and ocean circulation, extreme events), interacting with other drivers, on habitability, infrastructure, communities, livelihoods, loss of lives and assets and territories, infrastructure, ecosystems, coral reefs, access to resources, and institutional, social, economic, and cultural aspects.[32] Similarly, pointing to the rising global surface temperature, "World Scientists' Warning of a Climate Emergency," penned by William Ripple et al., issues an important warning: "Climate change is predicted to greatly impact marine, freshwater, and terrestrial life, from plankton and corals to fishes and forests ... These issues highlight the urgent need for action" (2020, 8).[33] In a more recent article,

[31] See Leslie, et al. (2022).
[32] See "Decision IPCC/XLV-2, Sixth Assessment Report (AR6). The Special Report on the Ocean and the Cryosphere in a Changing Climate," chapter 5: "Changing Ocean, Marine Ecosystems, and Dependent Communities": www.ipcc.ch/site/assets/uploads/sites/3/2022/03/07_SROCC_Ch05_FINAL.pdf.
[33] This was signed by 11,258 scientist signatories from 153 countries. See "Alliance of World Scientists" for further information: https://scientistswarning.forestry.oregonstate.edu. See also Lenton, et al. (2019), in which the authors note that "the evidence from tipping points alone

"Scientists' Warning of an Imperiled Ocean" (Georgian et al., 2022), the previous messages are reaffirmed with a more pronounced warning specifically focused on the ocean: "humanity must immediately and significantly alter our harmful trajectory in order to avoid irrevocably damaging our oceans in multiple ways that will further affect ocean health for both us and future generations" (2022, 1). Here the authors emphasize the "cumulative and interactive effects of multiple stressors" in the global ocean, which is subject to a "myriad of anthropogenic impacts ranging from resource extraction (e.g., fishing, oil and gas extraction, seabed mining), habitat deterioration and destruction, pollution, invasive species, and climate change" (2022, 1–2). According to the authors, one of the most harmful human activities is overfishing, especially bottom trawling, which is "the most damaging form of fishing due to its indiscriminate, large-scale, and destructive nature" (2022, 3). Their long list of anthropogenic activities include oil and natural gas extraction that damages the seafloor, generating sediment plumes; seabed mining; toxic waste materials; noise and light that significantly disturb, injure, and kill fragile benthic and pelagic communities; industrialization and urbanization of coastlines; global shipping traffic; aquaculture production; chemical pollution; greenhouse gas emissions; ocean deoxygenation; and alteration of ocean currents (2022, 3–4). Stating that if the oceans become less resilient, humanity will suffer the worst consequences, the authors then conclude with a warning message:

> If we do not alter our present trajectory, the accumulated damage may result in an irreversibly deteriorated ocean with considerably impaired functioning, aesthetics, and resilience, driving us toward a dead ocean lacking in life and biodiversity. Humanity must act quickly, with bold transformative actions to safeguard and restore healthy ecosystems in ocean habitats around the globe. (2022, 6)

This cautionary message invites transdisciplinary cooperation among scientists and scholars in the humanities and social sciences, calling for ethical responsibility that we owe to ourselves and all injured beings. Let me reiterate that any scientific or cultural paradigm that objectifies the Earth and commodifies wet matter is like a boomerang that eventually strikes its thrower, because, as David Rothenberg famously wrote about water, "We are made of it, we are enmeshed in it, we need it to survive, and it needs us to preserve it" (2002, xv). This is also

---

suggests that we are in a state of planetary emergency: both the risk and urgency of the situation are acute" (595). See also the inaugural issue of *Ecocene: Cappadocia Journal of Environmental Humanities* (2020): https://ecocene.kapadokya.edu.tr/index.php/ecocene/issue/view/1, which offers noteworthy responses from leading Environmental Humanities scholars to "World Scientists' Warning to Humanity: A Second Notice" (2017) and the "World Scientists' Warning of a Climate Emergency" (2020).

the fundamental message advocated by the blue humanities, encouraging us to think with water and all biotic entities living in the waters of this fragile planet.

All the oceanic challenges, the multiplying troubles in the saltwater habitats, and the warnings issued by world scientists necessitate new critical perspectives to contest the anthropocentric discourses still prevalent in the global cultural unconscious. A powerful counternarrative to anthropocentrism, as I have proposed in this Element, is the material ecocritical vision that acknowledges the affective agency of the ocean and recognizes its creative expressions. With its emphasis on storied seas, material ecocriticism can effectively denature anthropocentric narrative representations of the seascapes that are ingrained in our mental landscapes determining social behavior. Most importantly, storied seas invite us to collaborate in an aqueous imaginary that makes thinking with water possible and also imperative. Thinking with water, then, can lead to uncolonizable forms of water knowledge and reconfiguration of human–sea relationships. Another way is to re-envision the oceans in terms of "submarine immersions, multispecies others, feminist and Indigenous epistemologies, wet ontologies" (DeLoughrey 2019b, 22). Both paths invite us to test our habits of mind, our ecological imperatives, our conceptual frameworks, and our epistemologies so that building new oceanic imaginaries, formulating new discursive practices, and abandoning profit-based economic activities can become possible.

The World Ocean can no longer bear the pain of compounded changes with destructive effects on its geophysical properties and marine life itself. Part of the solution lies in saying a collective "no" to the advent of capitalistic practices, such as drilling the seabed for minerals or fossil fuels. The real solution, however, is in thinking with the ocean, which "involves asking *How would ways of speaking about (x) change if you were to displace or transport it to a different environmental context, like the ocean?*" (Jue 2020, 6; italics in the original). This important question posed by Melody Jue will inform the discussion to follow on the challenge of old paradigms and conventional or canonical narratives of water in all its forms.

4 Distressed Freshwaters

Concerned with ongoing chemical and biophysical transformations in the oceanic environments and climate change–induced biodiversity loss in the seas threatening the dynamism of aquatic existence, blue humanities scholars repeatedly argue that the "ontologies of the sea and its multispecies engagements" (DeLoughrey 2017, 32) are seriously disrupted by the financial interests of global capitalism and colonial logics. The same holds for freshwater ecosystems also subjected to the interests of the global finance system. Thus, "the rendering of freshwater as an extractable resource is equally underpinned by colonial logics, patriarchal formations, and financial adjustments" (Campbell and Paye 2020,1). The recent research in the blue humanities not only foregrounds the politics of such renderings but also asks us to change our modes of expression and ways of speaking about water because, as the basic element of all things, water is essential for all the ongoing processes of life, as Greek philosopher Thales reminds us from the sixth century BC.

Like all land animals, humans depend on lakes, ponds, rivers, fresh streams, marshes, and groundwaters, which, along with ice, constitute 99 percent of planetary freshwaters. According to limnologists, "[e]stimates of the global value of wetlands ($3.2 trillion per year) and rivers and lakes ($1.7 trillion per year) indicate the key importance of freshwaters to humans" (Dodds and Whiles 2010, 8). Due to this value index of freshwaters, their radical instrumentalization and destabilization through dams, enclosure, and drying compromise their ability to recover from the impacts of these stressors. Our water systems are, therefore, wounded in many ways, by "droughts and floods, aquifer depletion, groundwater contamination and salination" (Neimanis 2017, 5). All these problems which beset the hydrosphere have obvious socioeconomic consequences. The Water Resilience Coalition – a CEO-led initiative committed to reducing water stress by 2050 – for example, has announced that "the world will face a 40% shortfall in freshwater supply within 10 years,"[34] affecting the majority of the world's population. The UN Secretary-General Ban Ki-moon also stated that around 1.8 billion people will be facing water scarcity by 2025 simply because freshwater is distributed unevenly and much of it is polluted with human detritus, which the water's solvent properties cannot handle. As Tim Davie explains in *Fundamentals of Hydrology*, water's solvent properties only "allow the uptake of vital nutrients from the soil and into plants; this then allows the transfer of the nutrients within a plant's structure. The ability of water to dissolve gases such as oxygen allows life to be sustained within bodies of water such as rivers, lakes and oceans" (2002/2008, 2).

The story of water, and especially freshwater, is not only the story of living processes intermingled with the stories of all terraqueous organisms in the book of life, but also the story of our creative imagination, evoking curiosity, fear, and wonder with its symbolic power. Veronica Strang, too, affirms in *Water: Nature*

---

[34] See https://ceowatermandate.org/resilience/?gclid=EAIaIQobChMI1PGs84v6-gIVYoKDBx1SKQVxEAMYAiAAEgI_5PD_BwE.

and Culture that water does not only "flow through every organism" and our bodies, but also through our cultural imaginaries and all human practices:

> Water also permeates our emotions and imaginations, providing metaphors to think with. It flows through religious beliefs as well as political, economic and social practices. It is literally essential to every aspect of life, and it always has been. . . . Today, as conflicts over freshwater resources intensify, and even the great oceans are feeling the pressures of climate change and pollution, our bio-cultural relationship with water remains central not only to human well-being, but to that of every living species. (2015, 7–8)

Inscribed in geological time, the story of water is as old as the Earth itself. From the beginning of its formation 4.5 billion years ago, our planet's history has been written by water as the original scribe of planetary life and its many "geostories," to use the term coined by Latour (2014). Water (freshwater in particular, of course) is, therefore, the earliest architect of life on the planet, with its global hydrological cycle, which "consists of evaporation of liquid water into water vapour that is moved around the atmosphere. At some stage the water vapour condenses into a liquid (or solid) again and falls to the surface as precipitation" (Davie 2002/ 2008, 7). This cycle connects us corporeally to all aqueous communities, where, in Astrida Neimanis's insightful words, "the human infant drinks the mother, the mother ingests the reservoir, the reservoir is replenished by the storm, the storm absorbs the ocean, the ocean sustains the fish, the fish are consumed by the whale" (2012, 92). On the land surface, the sources of freshwater are rivers, lakes, reservoirs, creeks, ponds, streams, and wetlands, which keep life intact. The amount of water in these sources is never constant due to both the inflow of water to these water bodies from groundwater seepage and precipitation, and the outflow of water because of evaporation and drawing water from lakes and rivers by people.

Containing less than 1,000 milligrams per liter of dissolved solids, freshwater is a gift of life, but freshwaters are neither inexhaustible nor renewable sources.[35] The fact is that only 2.5 percent of all water on Earth is freshwater, and two-thirds of it is in ice caps, glaciers, and underground basins, "which means that less than 1 percent of the world's water is freshwater" (Nelson 2002, 20). This 1 percent of water is stored in the atmosphere and the soil, and in rivers, lakes, and marshlands. Lakes and swamps constitute 0.29 percent of the precious freshwater resource. Lake Baikal in Asia holds 20 percent of all surface water, and another 20 percent is in the Great Lakes in North America. All rivers combined contain about 0.006 percent of total

---

[35] See "Freshwater (Lakes and Rivers) and the Water Cycle." *USGS: Science for a Changing World.* June 8, 2018. 2018. www.usgs.gov/special-topics/water-science-school/science/fresh water-lakes-and-rivers-and-water-cycle.

freshwater reserves.[36] And wetlands contain only 0.03 percent of the world's water. Even though they are the most biologically rich of all ecosystems, provide protection against floods, and are sources of drinking water, about 50 percent of wetlands in the world have already been irremediably destroyed to make space for housing or for agricultural purposes. According to the 2007 EU report "Life and Europe's Wetlands," what causes this degradation is mostly "drainage for agriculture, infrastructure developments, forestation and malaria control, blocking and extraction of the water inflow, over-exploitation of groundwater resources, or the building of dams" (2007, 4). Since wetlands constitute a large part of the hydrological system, regulating climate and storing carbon, they are essential for the sustenance and well-being of local communities as well as for the flora and fauna that depend on them for nutrients. In their essay "Why a Marsh?" (2022), Daniel Wolff and Dorothy Peteet note that "if we want the communities of plants, birds, fish, and microbes that depend upon wetlands to continue (not to mention our own culpable species) – it's important to figure out how a marsh works, how it survives, why." Like marshes, ponds – as equally important components of the hydrosphere – suffer gravely from human pressures. Recent research shows that their capacity to preserve biodiversity, reduce flood risks, and improve runoff water quality has diminished as they continue to shrink in size. For example, 90 percent of ponds in Switzerland have been lost over the last two centuries, and less than a quarter of 800,000 ponds in the United Kingdom remain today. In Austria, 70 percent of ponds have also been lost (McGovan 2022).

All in all, the hydrosphere contains an estimated 1.5 billion cubic kilometers of water, and dry land itself is actually "made habitable by thousands of rivers, or is dotted with lakes, underlaid by huge reservoirs of groundwater, or covered by enormous amounts of water in frozen form" (Tvedt 2015/2021, 2). All this is vital for the maintenance of human, animal, and plant life. But overextraction of groundwater, drying of lakes and rivers, and hydraulic engineering projects that collect, store, and transport water for water resource management due to "increasing population pressure and possible changes in climate" (Davie 2002/2008, 152) have gained more momentum in the Anthropocene. The threats freshwater ecosystems (all ponds, rivers, creeks, streams, peats, marshes, swamps, and shoals) face is listed by limnologists Walter K. Dodds and Matt R. Whiles in *Freshwater Ecology: Concepts and Environmental Applications of Limnology*:

> Sediment, pesticide, and herbicide residues; fertilizer runoff; other nonpoint runoff; sewage with pathogens and nutrients; chemical spills; garbage dumping; thermal pollution; acid precipitation; mine drainage; urbanization; and

---

[36] For more information see *USGS*. Also, the NASA Earth Observatory page on water provides up-to-date information: https://earthobservatory.nasa.gov/topic/water.

habitat destruction are some of the threats to our water resources. Understanding the implications of each of these threats requires detailed understanding of the ecology of aquatic ecosystems. The effects of such human activities on ecosystems are linked across landscapes and encompass wetlands, streams, groundwater, and lakes. (2010, 10)

According to John. A Downing, too, these multiple forms of violence on freshwaters and an increasing population put "unprecedented pressure on water supplies" (2014, 216), limiting their rate of renewal as well as people's access to clean drinking water. As evidenced by the statistics shared by Water.org, a global nonprofit organization, 771 million people in the world – 1 in 10 – lack access to drinkable water.[37] If freshwater bodies continue to be the subjects of violence – "dredged and tamed through colonial and capitalist infrastructures" (Ranganathan 2022, 721), institutionalized by corporate market sector, and systematically polluted with household solvents, pesticides, cleaning agents, and agricultural fertilizers – the future seems fraught with problems, particularly in terms of food insecurity, public health crises, and sanitation issues triggered by water shortages, and floods and droughts intensified by climate change. Additionally, "the reductive rechoreography of vital waterways with dams, canals, and diversions" (Chen, MacLeod, and Neimanis 2013, 4) makes the renewal of inland waters almost impossible. This is because "the average global rate of renewal of inland waters via the hydrologic cycle is only 7% per year; therefore, only a small fraction of inland water can be used, spoiled, or polluted annually in a sustainable fashion" (Downing 2014, 216). This 7 percent renewal rate per year emphasizes the importance of freshwaters that deserve a fuller reading in the blue humanities through a reconsideration of their political, social, and ethical contexts, and through new narratives that allow for thinking with water. It is also important to formulate new epistemic strategies to account for the irrevocable ecological alterations in the hydrosphere. Thus, one can say with certainty that even though humans are the coda in the planet's evolutionary calendar as latecomers to the earth's phenomenal geostory, their influence is unprecedented.

And so, scientists call for "effective and equitable conservation of approximately 30% to 50% of Earth's land, freshwater and ocean areas" (IPCC 2022, 34). An equitable conservation requires effective politics and, as political scientist David Johns contends, must be focused on prevention rather than addressing symptoms because "[t]reating symptoms avoids the hard decisions and the risks that challenging the status quo inevitably carries" (2019, 3). But an effective conservation, first and foremost, begins with watery thinking – or

---

[37] See https://water.org/our-impact/water-crisis/global-water-crisis/.

thinking with water – that provides for more ethical relations with water habitats to ensure livable futures for both terrestrial and aquatic beings. And one way of developing ethical relations is "building care-based relationships with water, as partners in watery thinking" (Bailey-Charteris 2021, 436). To do so requires what Gaston Bachelard had called a *"water mind-set"* (1942/2006, 5; italics in the original) that envisions water in terms of the ancient Heraclitean flux. "A being dedicated to water," writes Bachelard, "is a being in flux" (1942/2006, 6). This kind of water mindset is not too different from the hydrological viewpoint material ecocriticism proposes for the blue humanities, acknowledging planetary waters as living, agentic entities with lively powers of expression. Using water-based imaginaries, in this sense, we become more attentive to the meaningfully articulate aquatic habitats and their inhabitants, and thus can attune to wet matter mostly by means of its storied dimension, recognizing water as a densely storied signifying subject and a site of narrativity. Seeing water from this perspective is like meeting wet matter halfway, as Karen Barad would say, for the way we are interrelated is always already infused with the stories we tell. We should, however, be careful, as Solnit (2023) advises us, about "what we take in and who's telling it, and what we believe and repeat, because stories can give power – or they can take it away." The "doom-soaked stories, for example," as Solnit calls them, cannot motivate people to change their relationship with the world, or even to imagine a better world. Hence the necessity for new stories that would motivate us "to do what it takes to make the world we need" (Solnit 2023).

The material ecocritical vision of storied waters fulfills this need for motivating stories and becoming better listeners as it offers us a chance to reimagine ourselves through our relations with aquatic beings no matter how different they may be from terrestrial beings, thus making possible the idea that storying of the world is not all too terrestrial. Everything aquatic embodies stories brought about by semiotic creativity inherent also in the watery worlds, which may not be easily perceptible to the human mind. These stories often unfold in the intersections of science studies and the blue humanities and can be read as narrative guidelines for the survival of all beings caught in the Anthropocene blues. In such narrative pathways, both the ambient and remote water environments and species can teach us noninvasive ways of relating to water worlds. In a way, the storied waters afford a much better and broader critical perspective on the plight of aquatic beings and the damaged waters than our existing stories and cognitive systems.

Crafting this kind of speculative and critical lens would, in my opinion, render visible the unforeseen relationalities of terrestrial and aquatic beings and their entangled tragedies. Maybe attending to the stories of aquatic life and writing new stories ourselves about our interdependencies can be instrumental in bending the curve of this decline in freshwater ecosystems. Let me quote Elaine Gan's words for further clarification: "We need to gather all the names, conceptual toolkits, and rallying cries together and take heed if we are to re-imagine and live worlds otherwise" (2017, 90). We also need to gather the kind of stories told by the watery commons and aqueous beings that can shape the futures to come, and rivers today are prime examples of such stories as they are granted legal rights and personhood.

4.1 Rivers

"Rivers are simply the places where water is most visible and alive," writes biologist Amy-Jane Beer in *The Flow* (2022, 32). But hydroelectric dams and megadams that transform free-flowing ecosystems into slow-flowing lake-like ecosystems[38] dim this understanding of water as a living entity. epitomizing ecological violence with disastrous environmental consequences. These include altered water quality; destruction of wetlands; declining food webs; loss of freshwater biodiversity;[39] redistribution of land, forest, or water resources; downstream farmers losing access to water; and displacement of people and, thus, violations of human rights (Schapper, Unrau, and Scheper 2021). Irrigated agriculture, for example, leads to diminishing harvests, causes land salination, and renders vast areas infertile. In sum, as epitomes of the hegemonic enclosure, megadams gravely disrupt hydrological flows in aquatic ecosystems. Kariba Dam on the banks of the Zambezi River between Zambia and Zimbabwe and Three Gorges Dam on the Yangtze River in China are familiar examples of exploitation caused by what Alexandra Campbell and Michael Paye call "hydraulic regimes," which, they state, "not only govern water, but consolidate the experience of inequality" (2020, 2). Thus, they add, megadams "transform river-waters into a commodity that can be pumped, stored, and directed in the service of capital" (2020, 3). When river waters become submersible merchandise manipulated by engineering projects, they lose their vitality and life-bearing spirit. The consequent changes in water depth throw the food webs into disarray, lessening the chances of survival for the endemic species that live in that river.

---

[38] See "Ecological Effects of Dams," Minnesota Department of Natural Resources, July 2013: www.minnehahacreek.org/sites/minnehahacreek.org/files/pdfs/projects/Ecological%20Effects %20of%20Dams%20July2013.pdf. Dams fragment rivers and streams and transform free-flowing ecosystems into slow-flowing, lake-like ecosystems For multiple environmental effects of dams, see M. K. Kaushik's conference paper, "Environmental Consequences of Large Dams" (Kaushik 2007).

[39] This happens when migrating fish meet barriers and migrating birds lose their breeding ground.

Transforming rivers into the Anthropocene's postnatural sites with such violent methods has grave repercussions for human lives as well. When, for example, Oahe Dam was built on the upper Missouri region in the 1950s, followed by the construction of five more dams on Missouri's main stem, the Sioux lands were all flooded "and more than nine hundred Native families were dislocated. Entangled in the cruel structures of control and manipulation of rivers, the Sioux families were deracinated – violently uprooted – from their river" (Ostler and Estes 2019, 99). This dramatic event demonstrates the tragic consequences of natural resource extraction for economic development through human-rights violation against Indigenous peoples and against the river itself through altering its flow – a river the Sioux have always honored as a living entity crucial for human and more-than-human survival. Such environmental injustices, then, carry violence across multispecies life, drastically altering human livelihoods and eliminating those of the nonhuman.

Another form of violence exerted on rivers is the pollution of pesticides, heavy metals, and hydrocarbons, all due to industrialization and urbanization policies, as in the case of Ergene River in Turkey's Thrace Region. Ergene's "basin area is 14,945.85 km^2 that consists of agricultural lands noted for high fertility" (Dedeoğlu 2019). With 11.325 km^2 of drainage areas, Ergene River Basin is comprised of the Çorlu and Ergene streams. About 1,000 textile factories flush their waste directly into the Ergene River and to its branches, forcing the Çorlu stream to cope with large amounts of toxic waste from textile and leather industries, as well as "wastewaters . . . from various other industries and municipalities" (Güneş, Güneş, and Talınlı 2008, 349). A laboratory analysis of toxicity levels in Ergene River indicated high levels of ammonia, chromium, sulfide and other heavy metals, and toxic dyes used in the textile industry.

Depleting oxygen levels, such drastic water pollution in rivers, inevitably reduces fish populations, disturbs the fishes' ability to find food, and causes "immunosuppression, reduced metabolism, and damage to gills and epithelia" (Austin 1998, 234S). It also impairs the photosynthesis processes of aquatic plants. Being so afflicted with chronic toxicity, Ergene River is listed among the twelve most polluted rivers in the world; others include the sacred Ganges River in India, contaminated with the dumping of raw sewage and chemicals; the Yellow River in China, into which chemical factories and coal mining industries release their toxic waste; the Marilao River in the Philippines, filled with heavy metals and waste from tanneries; the Mississippi river in the United States, overburdened with the constant release of harmful chemicals, such as mercury and arsenic, from industries, and from farmers who use nitrogen-based fertilizers; and the River Nile in Egypt, polluted with industrial and municipal wastewater and sewage release. As can be seen, the release of industrial waste into rivers is the biggest source of river contamination because of the hazardous chemicals and heavy elements, such as lead and mercury, that hamper the purifying cycle of water.

Yet another drastic result occurs when endocrine-disrupting synthetic chemicals flushed down toilets pass into rivers and cause gender change in fish and affect their behavior. Marked by the signs of lethal toxicity in rivers, the androgynous fish is a striking example of biotic alterations caused by synthetic chemicals. Because these chemicals "have the potential to cross the boundaries between species," they carry high risks for the human body as they can crucially alter "the hormone systems that shape our internal ecosystems of health, as well as our relationship with the broader ecosystems around us" (Langston 2010, 2), Considering rivers that are heavily exposed to "endocrine disruptors, neurotoxins, asthmagens, carcinogens and mutagens," Marietta Radomska and Cecilia Åsberg refer to this crisscrossing across bodies, land, and waterscapes as "toxic embodiment" (2020, 58).

For all these reasons, some countries around the world – such as Bolivia, Colombia, Ecuador, India, Mexico, and New Zealand – have implemented legal mechanisms and recognized the inalienable rights of rivers, acknowledging them as living subjects and agentic beings. This process began in 2017 with three rivers in different parts of the world that were given the status of legal persons. Other rivers then followed, being recognized as living subjects with intrinsic rights. In their article "When Rivers Have Rights: Case Comparisons of New Zealand, Colombia, and India," Craig M. Kauffman, and Pamela L. Martin list the rivers that have been granted legal status:

> In Ecuador, the Vilcabamba River became the world's first ecosystem to have its rights defended and recognized by a court ... New Zealand's Whanganui River (Te Awa Tupua) also has legal rights (New Zealand Government 2017). More recently, court rulings recognized the rights of the Atrato River in Colombia in 2016 and of the Ganga and Yamuna Rivers in India in 2017 (the Republic of Colombia Constitutional Court 2016; Uttarakhand High Court 2017). Internationally, a transnational network of lawyers and activists, coordinated by the Earth Law Center, are drafting a Universal Declaration of the Rights of Rivers (Earth Law Center 2017). (2018, 1)[40]

The declaration of the rights of rivers comes at a time when concerned communities across the world has seen how rivers "suffer from pollution, habitat destruction, overfishing, excessive diversions and a flurry of dam building"

---

[40] See http://files.harmonywithnatureun.org/uploads/upload585.pdf.

(Wilson and Lee 2019, 183). The cases of rivers that acquired rights illustrate the importance of giving "legal shape to the ways in which rivers are valued and understood – as sacred, living entities, as holistic and interconnected ecosystems, and as watersheds incorporating water, land, and forests" (Rights of Rivers 2017, 7). In the preamble to The Universal Declaration on the Rights of Rivers, we are reminded that rivers are essential to all life, and they not only play a vital role in the functioning of Earth's hydrologic cycle, but are also "sacred entities possessing their fundamental rights."[41] At the time this declaration was penned, the Whanganui River in New Zealand (called "Te AwaTupua" by the Māori) gained its legally recognized rights[42] and attracted much media attention in 2017, because its personhood "was established in association with the knowledge that local Māori ancestors exist as part of the river's water system" (Attala 2019,15). As a *person*, the river is now protected against hydroelectric projects.

This notion of water as being alive, as having personhood and its own inalienable rights, is not exclusive to the Māori but defines the cultures of many Indigenous peoples across the world, especially Native Americans, who never envisioned water bodies as inert exploitable resources. For example, the Mni Oyate, the Spirit Lake Tribe living on the Spirit Lake Dakota reservation in North Dakota, have always recognized "water as a legal person who is alive, who has agency and memory, and who holds legal standing" (Valandra 2019, 87). The Mni Oyate gained international recognition with their protest against a development project called the Dakota Pipeline (DAPL). As Mni Oyate scholar Edward Valandra remarks in his article "We are Blood Relatives: No to the DAPL" (2016): "water is alive – and therefore possesses personality or personhood ... Our definition challenges the West's anthropocentrism, which accords person/peoplehood only to humans. Hence the western way of life would both deny and defy water as having personhood."

It is important to note here that the western outlook, too, is changing, because in 2020, three years after the Whanganui River in New Zealand, a river in Europe – the Rhône River, originating from a melting glacier in the Swiss Alps – also gained personhood status through the "'Appel du Rhône,' a mobilization to recognize the juridical personhood of the river" (Luisetti 2022). A year later, in 2021, the Magpie River in Quebec, Canada, joined others in being granted personhood status. In the same year, during the IUCN World Conservation Congress held in Marseille, the participants agreed that

---

[41] The Universal Declaration of the Rights of Rivers (Earth Law Center 2017): www .rightsofrivers.org/#declaration.

[42] See Whanganui District Council website: www.whanganui.govt.nz/About-Whanganui/Our-District/Te-Awa-Tupua-Whanganui-River-Settlement.

freshwater ecosystems should be given legal protection. As living entities, rivers would now have legal standing in a court, so their free flows, preservation of biodiverse habitats, and protection from pollution can be guaranteed. This is because

> river systems are under extreme pressure. Many of the world's rivers suffer from extraordinary over-exploitation – through extraction, pollution, damming, alteration of natural flow regimes, and loss of water quality, and changes to riverine ecosystems, habitats and watersheds. As a result, freshwater vertebrate species are declining more than twice as fast as land-based and marine vertebrates. (Rights of Rivers 2017, 7)[43]

To protect the remaining rivers from these pressures, or to put an end to their disruptive encounters with our subversive nature, we need to acknowledge the rights of rivers and accept their personhood status and their agentic capacities, which help us reimagine them as fellow beings flowing in the same story as ours. Moreover, the legal rights given to rivers remind us of our mutual destiny, converging in the same naturalcultural realities. Recognizing the subjecthood of rivers is also recognizing them as narrative agencies whose stories trace maps of environmental contamination brought about by world-shaping regimes of power that only work to diminish the aquatic life with which we are interlocked in existential and often parasitic hydrological relations. When all the rivers in the world gain their legal rights, and when we make *thinking with water* our priority, we will find ourselves relating to them more ethically and less anthropocentrically. But this is all a matter of being listened to.

We must now seriously consider "the essential question of what is heard, and what is done about it" (Duckert 2017, 41) when the lakes speak and call for similar rights. Section 4.2 focuses on the voices of storied lakes and their narrative agencies that also need to be heard.

4.2 Lakes

As major components of the hydrosphere, and covering 4.2 million km^2 of Earth's surface, lakes are lentic habitats with stationary freshwaters, most of which date from the last glacial period. Using new data sources in 2006, John A. Downing and colleagues discovered that "[n]atural lakes and ponds $\geq$ 0.001 km^2 comprise roughly 2.8% of the non-oceanic land area" (2006, 2393). According to another study based on Landsat satellite imagery, "there are 117 million lakes larger than 0.002 km^2 in the world which collectively cover 3.7% of Earth's nonglaciated land area" (Dempsey 2014). These

---

[43] "The Rights of Rivers" Report, 2020: https://www.rightsofrivers.org.

117 million lakes "hold approximately 87% of the planet's liquid surface freshwater" (Woolway, Sharma, and Smol 2022, 1050). Also, according to evolutionary biologists James H. Thorp and Alan P. Covich, lentic habitats (wetlands and lakes) "contain 100 times as much water as stream and river habitats (=lotic)," and "most of the water is held within huge basins, such as the Laurentian Great Lakes of North America, Lake Baikal of Siberia, and Lake Tanganyika of East Africa" (2015, 23). They claim that "the combined relative importance of all wetlands, small ponds, creeks, and rivers is much greater than their volume percentages would otherwise indicate" (2015, 23).

As such, lakes are vital freshwater ecosystems, but because of the biological alterations and ecological disruptions they are undergoing they call for our attentiveness to their traumatic stories of pollution and exploitation. The most common limnological stressors that affect lakes are acidification and eutrophication (excessive nutrient supply), which result in the accumulation of metals (specifically lead) in sediments. Increasing metal toxicity in lentic ecosystems is mainly caused by modified zinc through dissolved organic matter, which becomes extremely poisonous for freshwater microalga (Price, et al. 2023). Moreover, when chemicals drain into streams and get transported downstream into lakes, fishermen, dairy farmers, and other local communities suffer the results.

Unlike lotic ecosystems, like rivers and streams with flowing waters, lakes (and wetlands, pools, ponds, and reservoirs) are lentic ecosystems with "no pervasive downhill flow" (Thorp and Covich 2015, 43) and contain a greater diversity of species. But, due to their changing chemical features, lentic fauna are becoming extinct. Thorp and Covich compare their rate of extinction "to the percentage loss of species from tropical forests," revealing how "intentional and accidental introductions of non-native, invasive species are affecting biodiversity and ecosystem processes" (2015, 40). The introduction of grass carp to the Neusiedlersee in Austria in the 1960s, for example, destroyed "the submerged vegetation, which represents an important spawning site for several fish species" (Jørgensen, et al. 2005, 47). Jørgensen and coauthors have also observed that in the Canadian province of Saskatchewan, "1.6 billion fish comprising 30 species were introduced to fresh and saline inland waters between 1900 and 1970" (2005, 47). The introduction of nonnative fish to lakes (i.e. the Alpine trout in high alpine lakes in Central Europe) affects not only the species diversity of fish but also the invertebrates. The health of a lake, these scientists note, depends on "having clean water, optimum algae growth, adequate oxygen levels and abundance and diversity of fish and bottom-dwelling invertebrates. Further, natural aquatic plants should flourish in appropriate habitats, and bottom habitat should be uncontaminated" (2005, 134). But pollutants from settlements with insufficient infrastructure and solid waste buried in landfills nearby contaminate both surface and groundwater.

A major threat that is more immediately recognizable comes from industrial pollution. This is specifically harmful for the breeding areas of migrating birds, such as flamingos. I would like to draw attention here to one specific example from a volcanic lake located in Turkey's Aegean region: Lake Acıgöl – "the bitter lake," in Turkish. As a saline lake, Acıgöl contains "a certain 12.5 million mt of sodium sulfate in the surface and subsurface brine (there is no solid deposit), with probable reserves of 70 million mt, and possible reserves of 82 million mt" (Garrett 2001, 128). Therefore, Lake Acıgöl has been used for commercial sodium sulfate production since 1953. To produce salt, the amount of water pumped from Acıgöl to the salt pans is approximately 6.77 million m^3 and the depth of salt pans is about 1.5 m, for 33.4 km^2 area, so a "total [of] 50.1 million m^3 of water was pumped from the lake to the salt pans for production" (Karaman, et al. 2011). Lake Acıgöl is also home to 178 bird species and is an important breeding ground for the Greater Flamingo as the dominant flamingo species here, but the ongoing sodium sulfate production activities, waste from the salt industry, and agricultural irrigation have decimated the number of these birds. They are losing their unique home for feeding and breeding, and thus their future, at a continual pace. Concerning the destruction of flamingo habitats, the four Turkish researchers quoted earlier announced in their conference paper that

> The Greater flamingos inhabit saline shallow water environments like salt pans, salt lagoons and alkaline lakes. The food of Greater flamingos is brine shrimp, larvae, blue-green and red algae, artemia, etc … Salt pans can also be considered as a feeding area where microorganisms (artemia salina) live although their life cycle is affected by the activities on salt pans. (Karaman, et al. 2011)

Lake Acıgöl is only one of the many representative cases of the ruination of lentic habitats and the violation of their inhabitants. Another noteworthy example is Lake Powell, a large reservoir located between southeastern Utah and northeastern Arizona in the United States, which is filled to 26 percent of its capacity due to intense drought. The Great Lakes (Superior, Michigan, Huron, Erie, and Ontario) that contain 20 percent of the world's freshwaters are also damaged by pollutants, including industrial wastes that flow to the lakes as heavy metals, and residential and agricultural waste products that decrease water quality and increase phosphorus levels. Similar to the oceans, when the concentrations of nitrogen and phosphorus increase, reducing oxygen levels, harmful algal blooms emerge that cause fish deaths. In order to restore lake ecosystems through the removal of toxic substances from impaired waters, the AOC program (the Great Lakes Areas of Concern) was established in the United

States, but the implementation was not consistent as the communities reported on "animal deformities, limited number of fish species, algae growth, and general sediment contamination" (Rentschler and Williams 2022, 1473; 1477). Nevertheless, the initiatives taken by local communities and organizations (such as the AOC program) to change the lakes' conditions through pollutant remediation and habitat restoration are important and must continue with effective community engagement and a sustained commitment to mitigation. This is evinced by the restoration of Mono Lake in California, which is known as a bird haven. If it weren't for the restoration project, the lake's ecosystem "would have collapsed ... under the combined pressure of water diversions and global warming" (Berwyn 2022). This project indicates that the protection of lentic ecozones must be a high priority for the health of all aquatic organisms, against the conceit of human greed.

Another major threat lakes face is rising water temperatures, or lake heatwaves, due to climatic shifts and anthropogenic stressors which, by intensifying the water cycles and decreasing the water elevation of the lake surface, endanger the lentic biodiversity. The consequences of heatwaves on lakes include "severe algal blooms ... mass die-off events ... and changes to the community composition of microscopic algae (phytoplankton), which form the bases of aquatic food webs" (Woolway et al., 2022, 1). In the opinion of Woolway and coauthors, when temperature anomalies occur in lakes and heatwaves exceed the thermal limits, lentic organisms may face local extinction as they may not be able to "adapt to extreme conditions" that involve loss of habitats and alterations in "food web dynamics" (2022, 8).

We need to recall that like the oceanic and lotic ones, lentic waterscapes remind us of our complicity in their tragedy as well as our interdependence and connectivity with their residents. The sonorous sounds of the bewildered flamingos from Lake Acıgöl and the dying fish in the Great Lakes only convey long-lasting sorrows of extinguished lives, which we cannot fathom without making connections and without understanding relational modes of existence. The stories of ongoing duress shared by the flamingos and the dramas of many migratory birds, fishes, and other vulnerable water-born species can only highlight our "failing connectivities" (Rose 2017, G52). If we can think with and through their grief and become, to quote conservation biologist Peter Warshall, better "hydro-citizens" (2001, 56), maybe we can rediscover our connectivities. To achieve this aim, we need to navigate these freshwater worlds with compelling stories that can stimulate our imagination to connect with the more-than-human aquatic communities. But these stories must be functionally contextualized in new modes of expression to convey knowledge about lentic ecosystem degradation. Heather Davis similarly suggests that "[w]e need modes of expression for the collective loss we are suffering through and venues to express the emotional toll of living in a diminished world" (2018, 65). Davis emphasizes the significance of art here, which, she says, offers "a range of discursive, visual and sensual strategies that are not confined by the regimes of scientific objectivity, political moralism or psychological depression" (2018, 64). So do literary narratives that render storied waters visible, readable, and relatable. Storied water reveals itself to the world through art, poetry, and fiction, and by the stories it tells as a narrative agency. Like those of rivers, the stories of lakes are not human-focused but concerned with the diminished lives of endemic species who are either fighting to survive – especially in the tragic sites of drained lakes – or have already vanished. The story of a dried lake in Turkey – Lake Amik – is one exemplary case for understanding the magnitude of damage precipitated by human activities.

Once located on the boundaries of the Hatay province (Southeastern part of Turkey) in the Amik Plain, Lake Amik is one of the saddest examples of a drained lake. Its story of falling from grace so many years ago still floods people's disturbed conscience but has barely touched the hearts of decision-makers. The process of drainage began in 1955 with the consent of the General Directorate of State Hydraulic Works (DSI) and was completed in 1980. The main reason for this decision was to eradicate malaria in the Amik Plain and to have usable land for agriculture, but ironically the new land created by drainage has caused not only ecological problems, such as disrupted weather patterns and floods, but also serious economic difficulties, such as fish habitat loss, depriving local people of their major source of income. Among other vicissitudes are the extinction of endemic fish species such as ray-finned fish and the disappearance of freshwater plants and migratory birds. Since the lake and its reed beds was an important resting site for about 200,000 migratory birds annually, and a breeding site for 48 bird species, such as waterfowls, white storks, and pelicans, they all lost their habitat during and after the drainage. The frog population, too, diminished as a result of draining. The lake was drained to increase land use to grow corn, black-eyed peas, cucumbers, and tomatoes specifically, but soil salination occurred in 5,000 ha of these lands, making agricultural activities highly problematic. The local people who earned their living through reed harvesting and fishing had to become farmers, but now they had to deal with soil salinity and floods. Additionally, excessive irrigation reduced the underground water level. Another poor decision was the building of an airport at the center of the drained lake, which faced high risks of recurrent flooding and bird collisions.[44]

---

[44] The runway of this airport was ripped apart by two successive devastating earthquakes in the region in February 2023, with magnitudes of 7.7 and 7.6.

In May 2001, for example, flooding caused loss of life, so the region was declared a disaster area. During the 2012 flooding of the Amik Plain (between January 27 and March 14), "an area of 13,000 hectares was affected and a total of 8465 ha of agricultural land, roads, bridges, settlements, and Hatay Airport [became] exposed to flood waters" (Üneş, et al. 2020, 2). As Turkish environmental scientists Emre Ozelkan, Zehra Damla Uca Avci, and Muhittin Karaman have observed: "Wetland destruction by draining, dredging, spoil deposition, and widening canals and navigating channels and impoundments for increasing agricultural regions have had significant local effects on wetland loss that are difficult or impossible to reverse" (2011, 28).

The drainage of Lake Amik is an ecological disaster, which is brought back to our cultural memory by Turkish novelist Y. Haluk Aytekin in his recent work of eco-fiction, *Ve Bir Göl Vardı Bir Zamanlar: Amik Gölünün Yok Edilişinin Öyküsü* (And There Was a Lake Once Upon a Time: The Story of Lake Amik's Destruction). Aytekin's novel vividly recounts the lake's obliteration. The lake, writes Aytekin, was once a "source of natural wealth with the flora and fauna it contained. Various birds, reptiles, mammals, amphibians, and insects lived in the lake and around the reed fields" (2017, 20).[45] Not capitalizing on water bodies as inert or expendable objects, this novel provides a trenchant critique of human decisions to destroy wetlands while making us aware of their lively agentic capacity. The novel has also contributed significantly to our conceptual map of the fragile lentic systems for it entails creative encounters with the lake's nonhuman inhabitants whose lives are irredeemably disrupted during the drainage process that took twenty-five years to complete. In a way, this novel is about remembering the "unhealed traumas" (Smith 2021, 245) of a lake that was once a significant ecological niche for aquatic, avian, and terrestrial species who suffered prolonged pain, anxieties, and traumas and endured a slow death. In the novel, they speak of the tragic tale of the demolition of their home and their complex but intimate relations with one another, highlighting the dire consequences of human misjudgment and political myopia at the time. By retrieving their stories, as sedimented in Amik's absent presence, Aytekin's novel makes them visible again. The novel is like a tribute to what James L. Smith writes about lakes: "Nothing deposited in the cultural memory of a lake ever truly goes away, reoccurring in social life with the shifting of political ecology and expressed through a prism of modes" (2021, 248). Indeed, everything that is imprinted in the cultural memory of Lake Amik has resurfaced with this novel, which has succeeded, to quote T. S. McMillin's words in *Strange Waters* (2022), in "kindl[ing] the will to rethink what we have done, and

---

[45] All translations from this novel, including the title, are mine.

inspire[d] us to imagine better courses of action." McMillin is right in claiming that "[l]iterature does this primarily by asking questions, and questions are an effective means by which we can unsettle ourselves, reexamine the world we inhabit." This is exactly what *Ve Bir Göl Vardı Bir Zamanlar* has achieved.

Lake Amik in Aytekin's novel never gets enlisted in aestheticized figurations to render its waters intangible and/or imaginary. On the contrary, the lake and its inhabitants – though anthropomorphized – are portrayed as lively, agentic, and sentient beings. When the lake gull Ka, for example, warns the fish and other species, such as pelicans, purple herons, frogs, reed cats, cranes, catfish, and eels, about the human decision to dry their only home, as readers we begin to think with them and to empathize with their impending fate. One of the endemic species living in the lake, the eel, tells Ka that this lake is the most important water habitat in the region:

> If this place dried up, thousands of us will die. If the seed fish, which are currently on the migration path, cannot find the lake when they arrive, they will starve to death. There are very few freshwater places in this area to feed such an eel population. When the time comes, we will embark on our last journey. If the lake disappears when our babies reach here, it would be a great disaster for them. I hope people realize the harm they are causing. (2017, 47)

The big catfish, Maho, who had been living in the lake for over thirty years, joins in the conversation:

> What do these humans want from us? As if it wasn't enough that they hunted us, now they will obliterate us all. There are as many as fifty-nine different fish species in this lake including us, the catfish, and the eels. So, what about all these fish?
>
> Seagull Ka: People don't care whether fish, birds, and other living things exist or not. Their only concern is to dry this lake. (2017, 49)

The important lesson we learn from these nonhuman characters that live in and around the lake is the relational logic of *becoming with* (Haraway 2008). They remind us of ecological communities of which we are also part because eventually the people living nearby are also influenced by the process of drainage, such as the fishermen who had to become farmers. Since the lake was once "a biotic world or swarm of agencies" (Yaeger 2010, 535), the tragic story of its dissolution is profoundly troubling, but at the same time it challenges us "to think through the literary and cultural implications" (Yaeger 2010, 538) of such lentic habitats. And literary representations of the death of a lake due to human misjudgment for economic profit are effective in making us aware of why water bodies should be given legal rights to flow or to remain intact and appreciated as agentic entities that are existentially entwined with us. Both parties shape each other in dynamic relationships that can be compellingly productive but also destructive in mutual *becoming with*. If this is so, "why then" – a vital question directed to the gull Ka by a strange water bird named Anhinga in Aytekin's novel – "are humans destroying our home and us?" The gull responds by raising its voice: "Why? You ask, why? Don't you know humans? They don't care at all about other beings. If necessary, they can burn the world for their small, vested interests" (2017, 51).

Despite their sabotaged agency, however, lakes like Amik continue to resound through us, enabling us to still feel their once vibrant flows and to hear the now-extinct voices of their occupants, as showcased with cogent examples in Aytekin's novel. How do we even function when freshwater bodies turn into arid landscapes? The challenge of the blue humanities is to put these fluid sites back into our mental and emotional maps and into literature and the arts, which help us redraw our relations between water flows, cultural practices, and wildlife habitats. Even if water has become the major actor of the Anthropocene troubles, it is still the very epitome of "the connections and integration of living processes" (Krause and Strang 2013, 96) and a symbol for life's intimate meanings, as it kindles our imagination and sparks poetic inspiration. Water's meanings are always colored by its "life-giving and life-threatening" (Krause and Strang 2013, 96) properties. This twofold nature of water emerges from the very fact that "[w]here the flow of water is reliable, clean, and plentiful, it fosters growth; where the flow is too much, too little, or too dirty, it wreaks havoc" (Barnes and Alatout 2012, 483). Thus, water's twofold identity needs to be considered within the larger framework of human imagination and material-discursive maps, and in combination with human–aquatic relations that require *thinking* collaboratively *with* aqueous agencies in their pain, struggles, and resilience. It is a kind of thinking, as explained by Thom van Dooren, "that inhabits complex multispecies worlds without the aid (and impediment) of simplistic divisions between the human and the nonhuman, the cultural and the natural" (2014, 147).

Taking this seriously, the blue humanities suggests that thinking beyond any single framework about the multilayered reality of water ecologies can liberate us from our objectifying attitude to all water bodies. Integral to this new thinking is a realization that our understandings necessarily proceed from disanthropocentrically shaped vantage points to dissolve any hydrocolonialist ideology and biopolitical strategies that give primacy only to human needs and human use of water. Thinking with water to honor water's vitality, however, does not mean turning a blind eye to human needs. On the contrary, access to safe water is a fundamental human right and a basic biological human need. At the same time, thinking with water enables us to envision water as a living narrative agency, with stories of its own and its own needs, which is the core claim of material ecocriticism. Thinking with the storied waters also incites us to rethink the categories via which we have reflected on water and its narratives. This model of thinking, in short, characterizes the discursive practices in the blue humanities that challenge received ideas about oceans and seas, rivers and lakes, and all waterscapes for that matter. They are all fluid-storied habitats that require a constant rethinking of their myriad meanings, their exigencies, and their critical physical conditions, which inevitably implicate human communities in various ways.

5 Epilogue

Acknowledging the ontological inseparability between lithic and liquid realms, and challenging "terracentric criticism" – a term American historian Markus Rediker uses in an interview (Bakker 2019) – the field of the blue humanities has produced alternative approaches to wet matter and thus altered the ways we think about our relationship with aquatic life. These approaches offer a general framework for thinking about water discourses, showing how more ecologically productive they can be. In this Element, with a view to the shift of the Earth's hydrological systems, I have proposed thinking with *storied* water as a new model that involves speculative knowledge practices to account for the creative expressions of marine and freshwater species, so they can be addressed as narrative agencies.

Part of my aim in this Element has been to draw attention to transdisciplinary models of research initiatives that the field of the blue humanities has adopted to offer desirable social and cultural solutions to the transformations occurring in all waterscapes. To raise critical awareness about these transformations, I find it particularly useful to highlight both the existential issues related to the physical realities and the symbolic configurations of water. This would allow for an acknowledgments of the reciprocal relationships between the aqueous and the terrestrial existence. This is to say that since its inception, the field has been both metaphorical and worldly in its research agendas. The unavoidability of speaking metaphorically about fluid sites is, in fact, self-evident as it is not possible to evade metaphoric language, but if metaphoric representations of waterscapes incite a mastering vision, they must be dismissed in the new poetics of water developing in the field. Although metaphoric relations especially with the oceans are still under scrutiny, I join other scholarly voices foregrounding their significance in developing conceptual knowledge. I concur with Melody Jue, for example, in insisting on the "fundamental reexamination of the underlying environmental poetics and metaphorics of our concepts and theoretical positions" (2020, 163).

Like metaphoric ones, the refiguring of land–water relations involves a twofold process by which water has shaped humanity (in terms of social and cultural codes) and humanity reshapes water habitats, often in either/or categories of friend or foe. Since the meanings that issue from this conjuncture are continuously redefined and can never be fixed, blue humanities scholarship has become heterogeneous in exploring the world's fluid sites and their material-symbolic relations among cultures, histories, and ecologies on a global scale. Therefore, it has become a dynamic field with a growing water poetics and new interpretive strategies that give prominence to aesthetic, literary, and scientific collaborations, waves of relations and connectivity in many academic fields, all of which necessitates thinking with water in what Barad terms "differential becoming" in terraqueous contexts (2007, 91).

Another point I want to emphasize in this Element is the significance of freshwater studies recently gaining more critical recognition in the blue humanities. Although much research in the field is still predominantly focused on critical ocean studies, with a strong emphasis on the escalating problems of saltwater habitats, as I have argued, the blue humanities has expanded its horizon by investing in the study of freshwaters. The implications of this expansion are evidently theoretical, historical, sociocultural, aesthetic, and literary. From the blue humanities perspective, the joint mission of salt and freshwater sciences, or oceanography and limnology, is advantageous because these two complementary scientific discourses enhance the field's transdiciplinarity and provide new insights for the literary and cultural narratives of wet matter. Drawing from these twin academic fields is also helpful in developing effective theories of aquatic processes. In other words, the field's multidisciplinary alliances with oceanography and limnology open a broader front for blue humanities scholars in addressing the complexity of hydrological problems with diverse theoretical assumptions made possible by transdisciplinary research protocols. Let me reiterate my theoretical perspective, which is material ecocriticism as instituted by Serenella Iovino and I. The connection to the material ecocritical conceptualization of wet matter here already implies a comprehensive theoretical and hydrocultural outlook. My suggestion is that perceiving water as a storied subject of an unfolding aquatic tale might lead to a mindset change and consequently transform overly detrimental capitalist practices that "lead up to an end-game of extinction" (Jagodzinski 2019, 112).

Since wet matter is never separable from social realities and cultural practices, the stories of its narrative agencies seem to me important and necessary as it is through disanthropocentric stories that the agentic liveliness of wet matter becomes conceivable and unsurprising for the reader. The point of bringing attention to the expressive agency of water and its aquatic beings is to enable cognizance of their innate rights to influence societal change. The storied waters in the Anthropocene unfold through the practice of thinking with water, which can liberate the mind from the shackles of anthropocentrism and indifference. This way of thinking begins with understanding that storytelling, as Bruno Latour affirms, "is not just a property of human language, but one of the many consequences of being thrown in a world that is, by itself, fully articulated and active" (2014, 13). Material ecocriticism has made this point central to its theoretical stance, claiming that there are stories encoded in all material forms, making matter storied. In this view, creativity is not only a human affair: storytelling is perceived as an enactment of creative becoming in everything/being that exists. Whether solid or fluid in form, storied matter allows for a vision in which matter is acknowledged as lively and agentic, communicating its stories, all of which are about worlding, storying the world, and reality-making, as much as reflecting on these processes. Life itself, whether underwater or on land, is always a cocreation on a collective level and a site of narrativity endowed with diverse signs and meanings, making every being, thing, and force storied in the lithosphere, biosphere, hydrosphere, and atmosphere.

As I have discussed in this Element, coral reefs tell stories of oceanic warming, acidified seawater, and chemical pollution. The plastic-choked birds on Midway Island are the narrators of their traumatic lives and slow deaths. The sea snot known as mucilage – a type of sea algae that has overgrown in the Sea of Marmara – tells the story of the suffocation of marine life caused by rising water temperatures, human waste products, and excessive fishing. The endangered flamingos of Acıgöl narrate their tragic tales brought about by "uncontrolled production of salt, wastes of salt industry and residential areas, [and] agricultural irrigation activities" (Karaman, et al. 2011). I am also reminded of the Mystic River in Boston, filled with anoxic bacteria, as a narrative agency itself telling stories of its own mutability, its tensions, and its biochemically changing water quality critically affecting not only the fish, such as herring, but also plants like water lilies. The construction of the Amelia Earhart dam here transformed "the Mystic from a tidal river into a freshwater river" (Scaramelli 2013, 152). Stories of fish and the water lily in the Mystic River demonstrate that when waterflow is changed "with canalized tributaries," it inevitably has adverse effects on "the life-enabling biochemical properties of water . . . making it difficult for water beings to live" (Scaramelli 2013, 156). The storied lakes also foreground similar ecological decline, as we have seen in the exemplary story of Lake Amik's death, which is a heartbreaking tale. So are the whispers of its narrative agencies, most of which disappeared since the lake's drainage: endemic fish, migratory birds, and the lakeshore reeds that were once the important components of Lake Amik's ecosystem and the local climate. But their stories still circulate in the cultural memories of the region. These stories enable us to see a bygone lake from nonhuman vantage points, and to understand its purpose that, in general, is obscured from our dimmed human vision.

Reading storied waters this way, with aquatic nonhumans featuring as narrative agencies, and thus through the stories told by these lively life-forms subjected to agricultural pressures, industrial waste, badly maintained infrastructures, and foolish political decisions, can help us redefine our connections to water worlds. These stories call on us to reflect on the consequences of human activities in waterscapes in affective ways. This is basically a call to heart-searching, which is best expressed by the narrator in John Lane's poem "EROSION," who alerts the reader with the following question of why we need to do such a search:

> why search unless something
> is really lost, and what is, that is the question, begs all
> those useless trivia answers, conundrums, cacophonies
> information feeding our brains, fogging the windshield
> of what matters. (2017, 11)

What really matters here is that instead of becoming demoralized or desensitized by the dismal stories of oceans, seas, lakes, and rivers, and paying only cursory attention to their intrinsic value, we need to recognize them as signifying agents and think with them. In the blue humanities, this is facilitated by new narratives (such as the fictional texts discussed earlier) that demonstrate how *thinking with* can be possible, and by artworks such as the Crochet Coral Reef project, which has configured new ways of thinking together. These works also dehierarchize our conceptual categories that have determined our oppressive social, cultural and political practices.

To recapitulate the main point of this Element, "water is good to think with" (Attala 2019, 53), which has indeed brought about a major shift in the way in which we engage with aquatic ontologies in deeper ways so that all mastering visions dissolve in this process. In thinking with water, we can learn to give emphatic value to an experience of what Donna Haraway calls "response-ability," which she explains as "not something that you just respond to," but "as inheriting obligations we did not and cannot choose, but which we must respond to" (2015, 257, 261). The stories told by water's narrative agencies that presage what will happen if we continue to adhere to human hubris can help us cultivate and facilitate our response-ability. Another way of cultivating response-ability can be through a practice termed "reading with water" by Polish art critic Karolina Majewska-Güde, who advocates an aqueous reading that "is embedded in the idea of attentive and vulnerable listening/looking" (2021, 358). The key here is being *attentive* and *vulnerable listening* to water-scapes while experiencing the capacity to be response-able "that is also collect-ive knowing and doing, an ecology of practices. Whether we asked for it or not, the pattern is in our hands" (Haraway 2016, 34). With such an internalized exposition of declining ecological conditions in all waterscapes, we can perhaps inspire a self-conscious awareness of storied waters in the general mindset. A livable world, to quote Rebecca Solnit again, "is all about what stories we tell and whose stories are heard" (2023). Stories can change our customary ways of thinking about troubled waters and help us discover deeper meanings about our entangled relations with water that gave us and all that is biological the gift of life on this planet. Thus, though it may sound like a bold claim, I want to conclude by affirming that solutions lie in the new stories we tell, and in stories told by aquatic narrative agencies that enable us to think with water.

About the Author

A professor of Environmental Humanities, Serpil Oppermann is director of the Environmental Humanities Center at Cappadocia University. She is one of the signatories of the "World Scientists' Warning to Humanity: Second Notice" (2017) and the "World Scientists' Warning of Climate Emergency" (2020). Her work explores the relationships of human and more-than-human environments from the intersecting perspectives of natural sciences and environmental humanities. She has published widely on ecocritical theory, environmental humanities, posthumanism, ecofeminism, and the Anthropocene. Her most recent book, *Ecologies of a Storied Planet in the Anthropocene*, was published in 2023.

References

Alaimo, S. 2019. "Introduction: Science Studies and the Blue Humanities." *Configurations* 24(4): 429–432.

Allison, E. H., J. Kurien, Y. Ota, et al. 2020. "The Human Relationship with Our Ocean Planet." Blue Paper. Washington, DC: World Resources Institute, pp. 1–74. https://oceanpanel.org/human-relationship-our-ocean-planet/.

Anderson, J., A. Davies, K. Peters, and P. Steinberg. 2023. "Introduction: Placing and Situating Ocean Space(s)." In K. Peters, J. Anderson, A. Davies, and P. Steinberg, eds. *The Routledge Handbook of Ocean Space*. New York: Routledge, pp. 4–16.

Appeltans, W., S. T. Ahyong, G. Anderson, et al. 2012. "The Magnitude of Global Marine Species Diversity." *Current Biology* 22(23): 2189–2202.

Attala, L. 2019. *How Water Makes Us Human: Engagements with the Materiality of Water*. Cardiff: University of Wales Press.

Austin, B. 1998. "The Effects of Pollution on Fish Health." *The Society for Applied Microbiology* 85(S1): 234S–242S. First published online Nov. 5, 2010. https://doi.org/10.1111/j.1365-2672.1998.tb05303.x.

Aytekin, H. Y. 2017. *Ve Bir Göl Vardı Bir Zamanlar: Amik Gölünün Yok Edilişinin Öyküsü*. Ankara: Gece Kitaplığı.

Bachelard, G. 1942/2006. *Water and Dreams: An Essay on the Imagination of Matter*. Trans. E. R. Farrell. Dallas: The Dallas Institute of Humanities and Culture.

Bailey-Charteris, B. 2021. "Revealing the Hydrocene: Reflections on Watery Research." *Przegląd Kulturoznawczy* 2(48): 431–445. www.ceeol.com/search/article-detail?id=1012073.

Bakker, J. M. 2019. "Offshore: Descending into the Blue Humanities." *Counterpoint: Navigating Knowledge*. Blogspot. November 6, 2019. www.counterpointknowledge.org/offshore-descending-into-the-blue-humanities/.

Bakker, M. 2012. "Water: Political, Biopolitical, Material." *Social Studies of Science* 42(4): 616–623.

Balcı, A. 2021. "Yaşar Kemal's Ecopoetics of the Sea." In S. Oppermann and S. Akıllı, eds. *Turkish Ecocriticism: From Neolithic to Contemporary Timescapes*. Lanham: Lexington Books, pp. 115–127.

Barad, K. 2007. *Meeting the Universe Halfway: Quantum Physics and the Entanglement of Matter and Meaning*. Durham: Duke University Press.

Barnes, J., and S. Alatout. 2012. "Water Worlds: Introduction to the Special Issue of Social Studies of Science." *Social Studies of Science* 42(4): 483–488.

Barthes, R. 1977. "Introduction to the Structural Analysis of Narratives." In *Image Music Text*. Trans. S. Heath. London: Fontana Press, pp. 79–124.

Baud, A., J. P. Smol, and C. Meyer-Jacob. 2023. "The Impacts of Whole-Lake Acidification and Eutrophication on the Accumulation of Lead in Sediments from Manipulated Lakes in the Experimental Lakes Area (IISD-ELA)." *Environmental Pollution* 317(11): 1–11.

Beer, A.-J. 2022. *The Flow: Rivers, Waters and Wildness*. London: Bloomsbury Wildlife.

Bélanger, P. 2014. "Editor's Note." *Wet Matter*: Harvard Design Magazine 39 (F/W): 1–3. www.harvarddesignmagazine.org/issues/39.

Bencke, I., and J. Bruhn. 2022. "Introduction." In Ida Bencke and Jørgen Bruhn, eds. *Multispecies Storytelling in Intermedial Practices*. Santa Barbara: Punctum Books, pp. 9–20.

Bennet, J. 2010. *Vibrant Matter: A Political Ecology of Things*. Durham: Duke University Press.

Berwyn, B. 2022. "How Decades of Hard-Earned Protections and Restoration Reversed the Collapse of California's Treasured Mono Lake." *Inside Climate News*: Science. October 30, 2022. https://insideclimatenews.org/news/30102022/mono-lake-california-restoration/.

Berx, B., D. Volkov, J. Baehr, et al. 2021. "Climate-Relevant Ocean Transport Measurements in the Atlantic and Arctic Oceans." *Oceanography* 43(4): 10–11.

Besson, F. 2021. "Nature's Speech and Storytelling: The Voice of Wisdom in the Nonhuman." In B. Meillon, ed. *Dwellings of Enchantment Writing and Reenchanting the Earth*. Lanham: Lexington Books, pp. 67–84.

Biro, A. 2013. "River-Adaptiveness in a Globalized World." In C. Chen, J. MacLeod, and A. Neimanis, eds. *Thinking With Water*. Quebec: McGill-Queen's University Press, pp. 166–184.

Blum, H. 2010. "The Prospect of Oceanic Studies." *PMLA* 125(3): 670–677.

Bradley, J. 2017. "Writing on the Precipice." *Sydney Review of Books*. February 21, 2017. https://sydneyreviewofbooks.com/essay/writing-on-the-precipice-climate-change/.

Brayton, D. 2012. *Shakespeare's Ocean: An Ecocritical Exploration*. Virginia: University of Virginia Press.

Bystrom, K., and I. Hofmeyr. 2017. "Oceanic Routes: (Post-it) Notes on Hydro-Colonialism." *Comparative Literature* 69(1): 1–6.

Campbell, A. 2017. "Sound Waves: 'Blue Ecology' in the Poetry of Robin Robertson and Kathleen Jamie." *Études Écossaises* 19. https://doi.org/10.4000/etudesecossaises.1199.

Campbell, A., and M. Paye. 2020."Water Enclosure and World-Literature: New Perspectives on Hydro-Power and World-Ecology." *Humanities* 9(106):1–15.

Campling, L., and A. Colás. 2021. *Capitalism and the Sea: The Maritime Factor in the Making of the Modern World*. London: Verso Books.

Carabine, K. 1998. "Introduction and Notes." In J. Conrad, *Three Sea Stories: Typhoon, Falk and The Shadow-Line*, ed. K Carabine. Chatham: Wordsworth Editions Ltd.

Carson, Rachel. 1951/1961. *The Sea Around Us*. New York: Oxford University Press.

Center for Biological Diversity. 2017. "Oceanic Plastic Pollution: A Global Tragedy for Our Oceans and Sea Life." www.biologicaldiversity.org/campaigns/ocean_plastics/.

Chaturvedi, S. 2022. "Maritime Regionalism and 'Inclusive Development': Opportunity and Challenges before Bangladesh in Anthropocene." *Journal of International Relations* 15(1–2): 159–184.

Chen, C., J. MacLeod, and A. Neimanis. 2013. "Introduction." In C. Chen, J. MacLeod, and A. Neimanis, eds. *Thinking with Water*, Quebec: McGill-Queen's University Press, pp. 3–22.

Cheng, L., J. Zhu, J. Abraham, et al. 2019. "2018 Continues Record Global Ocean Warming." *Advances in Atmospheric Sciences* 36: 249–252.

Cohen, A. L., and M. Holcomb. 2009. "Why Corals Care About Ocean Acidification: Uncovering the Mechanism." *Oceanography* 22(4): 118–127.

Cohen, J. J. 2015. *Stone: An Ecology of the Inhuman*. Minneapolis: University of Minnesota Press.

Cohen, J. J., and S. Foote. 2021. "Introduction: Climate Change/Changing Climates." In J. J. Cohen and S. Foote, eds. *The Cambridge Companion to Environmental Humanities*. New York: Cambridge University Press, pp. 1–10.

Cohen, M. 2010a. *The Novel and the Sea*. Princeton: Princeton University Press.

Cohen, M. 2010b. "Literary Studies on the Terraqueous Globe." *PMLA* 125(3): 657–662.

Coole, D., and S. Frost. 2010. "Introducing the New Materialisms." In D. Coole and S. Frost, eds. *New Materialisms: Ontology, Agency, and Politics*. Durham: Duke University Press, pp. 1–43.

Cory, J. S. 2019. "Anthropocene Blues by John Lane." *The Goose* 17(2). https://scholars.wlu.ca/thegoose/vol17/iss2/20.

Cottey, A. 2022. "Climate and Nature Emergency: From Scientists' Warnings to Sufficient Action." *Public Understanding of Science* 31(6): 818–826.

Danovaro, R., P. V. R. Snelgrove, and P. Tyler. 2014. "Challenging the Paradigms of Deep-Sea Ecology." *Trends in Ecology & Evolution* 29(8):465–474.

Davie, T. 2002/2008. *Fundamentals of Hydrology.* Taylor & Francis e-Library.

Davis, H. 2018. "Art in the Age of the Anthropocene." In R. Braidotti, ed., *Posthuman Glossary.* London: Bloomsbury, pp. 63–65.

Davis, H. 2022. *Plastic Matter.* Durham: Duke University Press.

Dedeoğlu, Ç. 2019. "Cosmology of the Ergene River Pollution." *Arcadia* 38. www.environmentandsociety.org/arcadia/cosmology-ergene-river-pollution.

DeLoughrey, E. 2017. "Submarine Futures of the Anthropocene." *Comparative Literature* 69(1): 32–44.

DeLoughrey, E. 2019a. *Allegories of the Anthropocene.* Durham: Duke University Press

DeLoughrey, E. 2019b. "Toward a Critical Ocean Studies for the Anthropocene." *English Language Notes* 57(1): 21–36.

DeLoughrey, E. 2023. "Mining the Seas: Speculative Fictions and Futures." In I. Braverman, ed. *Laws of the Sea: Interdisciplinary Currents.* New York: Routledge, pp. 145–163.

Dempsey, C. 2014. "How Many Lakes are There in the World?" *GeoGraphyrealm,* October 1, 2014. www.geographyrealm.com/many-lakes-world/.

Dewey, C. D. 2014. "Crafty Sailors, Unruly Seas: Margaret Cohen's Oceanic History of the Novel." *Criticism* 56(4): 861–870.

Dobrin, S. I. 2021. *Blue Ecocriticism and the Oceanic Imperative.* New York: Routledge.

Dodds, W. K., and M. R. Whiles. 2010. "Why Study Continental Aquatic Systems?" In W. K. Dodds, and M. R. Whiles, eds. *Freshwater Ecology: Concepts and Environmental Applications of Limnology.* Burlington: Elsevier Academic Press, pp. 1–18.

Doney, S., W. M. Balch, V. J. Fabry, and R. A. Feely. 2015. "Ocean Acidification: A Critical Emergent Problem for the Ocean Sciences." *Oceanography* 22(4): 16–25.

Downing, J. A. 2014. "Limnology and Oceanography: Two Estranged Twins Reuniting by Global Change." *Inland Waters* 4(1): 215–232.

Downing, J. A., Y. T. Prairie, J. J. Cole, et al. 2006. "The Global Abundance and Size Distribution of Lakes, Ponds, and Impoundments." *Limnology and Oceanography* 51(5): 2388–2397.

Duckert, L. 2017. *For All Waters: Finding Ourselves in Early Modern Wetscapes.* Minneapolis: University of Minnesota Press.

Ecocene: Cappadocia Journal of Environmental Humanities. Inaugural Issue (2020). https://ecocene.kapadokya.edu.tr/index.php/ecocene/issue/view/1.

"Ecological Effects of Dams." Minnesota Department of Natural Resources. July 2013. https://www.minnehahacreek.org/sites/minnehahacreek.org/files/pdfs/projects/Ecological%20Effects%20of%20Dams%20July2013.pdf.

Eliot, T. S. 1930/1958. *The Waste Land and Other Poems*. New York: Harvest Books.

Estok, S. C. 2021. "Introduction to the Special Cluster 'Never Really Far From Us – Epidemics and Plagues in Literature.'" *Neohelicon* 48: 435–442.

EU Report on Wetlands. 2007. "Life and Europe's Wetlands: Restoring a Vital Ecosytem." https://ec.europa.eu/environment/archives/life/publications/life publications/lifefocus/documents/wetlands.pdf.

European Commission, Directorate-General for Environment, Silva, J., Jones, W., Phillips,L. 2008. "Life and Europe's Wetlands – Restoring a Vital Ecosystem." Publications Office. https://data.europa.eu/doi/10.2779/22840, pp. 1–65.

Federman, R. 1993. *Critifiction: Postmodern Essays*. New York: State University of New York Press.

Frank, Søren. 2022. *A Poetic History of the Oceans Literature and Maritime Modernity*. Leiden: Brill.

Gabbott, S., S. Key, C. Russell, Y. Yohan, and J. Zalasiewicz. 2020. "The Geography and Geology of Plastics: Their Environmental Distribution and Fate." In T. M. Letcher, ed. *Plastic Waste and Recycling: Environmental Impact, Societal Issues, Prevention, and Solutions*. London: Elsevier, Academic Press, pp. 33–63

Gan, E. 2017. "Timing Rice: An Inquiry into More-than-Human Temporalities of the Anthropocene." *New Formations* 92: 87–101.

Gan, E., A. L. Tsing, H. Swanson, and N. Bubandt. 2017. "Introduction: Haunted Landscapes of the Anthropocene." In A. L. Tsing, H. Swanson, E. Gan, and N. Bubandt, eds. *Arts of Living on a Damaged Planet: Ghosts and Monsters of the Anthropocene*. Minneapolis: University of Minnesota Press, pp. G1–G14.

Garrett, D. E. 2001. *Sodium Sulfate: Handbook of Deposits, Processing, Properties and Use*. San Diego: Academic Press.

Gelpke, N. 2015. Preface. *World Ocean Review* 4: Sustainable Use of Our Oceans – Making Ideas Work.

Genesy, C. 2019. Review of *Anthropocene Blues*: Poems. By John Lane." *ISLE* 26(1): 248–249.

Gentner, D., and M. Jeziorski. 1993. "The Shift from Metaphor to Analogy in Western Science." In A. Ortony, ed. *Metaphor and Thought*. Cambridge: Cambridge University Press, pp. 447–480.

Georgian, S., S, Hameed, L. Morgan, et al. 2022. "Scientists' Warning of an Imperiled Ocean." *Biological Conservation* 272(109595): 1–8.

Gillis, J. R. 2013. "The Blue Humanities." *Humanities* 34(3):n.p. May/June 2013. www.neh.gov/humanities/2013/mayjune/feature/the-blue-humanities.

Gilroy, Paul. 1993. *The Black Atlantic: Modernity and Double Consciousness.* Cambridge: Harvard University Press.

Glick, D. 2019. "The Big Thaw." *National Geographic.* September 23, 2019. www.nationalgeographic.com/environment/global-warming/big-thaw/.

Gruber, N., D. Clement, B. Carter, et al. 2019. "The Oceanic Sink for Anthropogenic CO_2 from 1994 to 2007." *Science* 363(6432): 1193–1199.

Güneş, E. H., Y. Güneş, and İ. Talınlı. 2008. "Toxicity Evaluation of Industrial and Land Base Sources in a River Basin." *Desalination* 226: 348–356.

Hablützel, P. I., I. Rombouts, N. Dillen, et al., 2021. "Exploring New Technologies for Plankton Observations and Monitoring of Ocean Health." *Oceanography* 34(4): 20–25.

Hall, S. 1997/2002. "The Work of Representation." In S. Hall, ed. *Representation: Cultural Representations and Signifying Practices.* London: Sage, pp. 15–64.

Haraway, D. 1997. *Modest Witness @ Second Millenium. Female Man Meets Oncomouse.* New York: Routledge.

Haraway, D. 2008. *When Species Meet.* Minneapolis: University of Minnesota Press.

Haraway, D. 2015. "Anthropocene, Capitalocene, Chthulhucene: Donna Haraway in conversation with Martha Kenney." In H. Davis and E. Turpin, eds. *Art in the Anthropocene: Encounters Among Aesthetics, Politics, Environments and Epistemologies.* London: Open Humanities Press, pp. 255–270.

Haraway, D. 2016. *Staying with the Trouble: Making Kin in the Chthulucene.* Durham: Duke University Press.

Hau'ofa, E. 2008. *We are the Ocean: Selected Works.* Honolulu: University of Hawai'i Press.

Head, M. J., J. A. Zalasiewicz, C. N. Waters, et al. 2022. "The Anthropocene is a Prospective Epoch/Series, not a Geological Event." *Episodes: Journal of International Geoscience.* August 15, 2022: 1–10. https://doi.org/10.18814/epiiugs/2022/022025.

Hekinian, Roger. 2014. *Sea Floor Exploration: Scientific Adventures Diving into the Abyss.* New York: Springer.

Hessler, S. 2020. "Tidalectic Curating." *Journal of Curatorial Studies* 9(2): 248–270.

Hofmeyr, I. 2019. "Literary Ecologies of the Indian Ocean." *English Studies in Africa* 62(1): 1–7.

Horden, P., and N. Purcell. 2006. "The Mediterranean and 'the New Thalassology.'" *American Historical Review* 111(3): 733–736.

Iovino, S. 2021. *Italo Calvino's Animals: Anthropocene Stories.* Cambridge: Cambridge University Press.

Iovino S., and S. Oppermann. 2014. "Introduction: Stories Come to Matter." In S. Iovino and S. Oppermann, eds. *Material Ecocriticism*. Bloomington: Indiana University Press., pp. 1–17.

IPCC. 2019. "Special Report on the Ocean and Cryosphere in a Changing Climate." www.ipcc.ch/srocc/.

IPCC Sixth Assessment Report on "Climate Change." 2022. Impacts, Adaptation, and Vulnerability. Chapter 3., pp. 3–235. www.ipcc.ch/report/ar6/wg2/.

Jagodzinski, J. 2019. "Into the Dark Blue: A Medi(t)ation On The Oceans – Its Pain, Its Wonder, Its Wild, and Its Hope." *symploke* 27(1–2): 111–138.

Johns, D. 2019. *Conservation Politics: The Last Anti-Colonial Battle*. Cambridge: Cambridge University Press.

Jordan, C. 2009. *Midway: Message from the Gyre*. Documentary.

Jørgensen, S. E., H. Löffler, W. Rast, and M. Straškraba, eds. 2005. *Developments in Water Science* 54: *Lake and Reservoir Management*. Amsterdam: Elsevier. Chapter 2, pp. 1–41; chapter 3, pp. 107–168.

Jue, M. 2020. *Wild Blue Media: Thinking Through Seawater*. Durham: Duke University Press.

Jue, M., and R. Ruiz. 2021. "Thinking with Saturation Beyond Water: Thresholds, Phase Change, and the Precipitate." In M. Jue and R. Ruiz, eds. *Saturation: An Elemental Politics*, Durham: Duke University Press, pp. 1–26.

Kabaağaçlı, C. Ş. (The Fisherman of Halicarnassus).1961. "Adalar Denizi Akdeniz" (The Sea of Islands: Mediterranean). *Mavi Sürgün* (*The Blue Exile*). Istanbul: Bilgi, 2003, pp. 239–246.

Kabaağaçlı, C. Ş. 1972. Prologue. *Ege'den Denize Bırakılmış bir Çiçek* (*A Flower Left to the Aegean Sea*). Istanbul: Bilgi.

Kane, I. A., and A. Fildani. 2021. "Anthropogenic Pollution in Deep-Marine Sedimentary Systems – A Geological Perspective on the Plastic Problem." *Geology* 49(5): 607–608.

Karaman, M., Z. D. Uca Avci, I. Papila, and E. Ozelkan. 2011. "The Analysis of Destruction in Flamingo Habitat of Acıgöl Wetland." Conference paper. 34th International Symposium on Remote Sensing of Environment, Sidney. April 2011. www.researchgate.net/publication/268811746_The_Analysis_of_Destruction_in_Flamingo_Habitat_of_Acigol_Wetland.

Kauffman, C. M., and P. L. Martin. 2018. "When Rivers Have Rights: Case Comparisons of New Zealand, Colombia, and India." http://files.harmony withnatureun.org/uploads/upload585.pdf.

Kaushik, M. K. "Environmental Consequences of Large Dams." Conference paper. December 2007. Conference: International Congress of Environmental Research (ICER-07). At Govt. Geetanjali Girls P.G. College, Bhopal. www.researchgate .net/publication/305724001_Environmental_Consequences_of_Large_Dams.

Kemal, Yaşar. 1978/1990. *The Sea-Crossed Fisherman*, trans. Thilda Kemal. London: Minerva.

Kidwell, D. 2015. "Oceanic Continental Margin Dead Zones Emerge as Threats to Coastal Waters." *National Centers for Coastal Ocean Science*. https://coastalscience.noaa.gov/news/oceanic-continental-margin-dead-zones-emerge-threats-coastal-waters/.

Kıryaman, E. 2019. "The Land Ethic and Human-Sea Relations in Yashar Kemal's *The Sea-Crossed Fisherman* and Sait Faik Abasıyanık's 'Sınağrit Baba' and 'Death of the Dülger.'" In B. P. Robertson, E. V. Kobeleva, S. W. Thompson, and K. D. Weddle, eds. *The Sea in the Literary Imagination: Global Perspectives*. Newcastle upon Tyne: Cambridge Scholars, pp. 107–122.

Krause, F, and V. Strang. 2013. "Introduction to Special Issue: 'Living Water.'" *Worldviews: Global Religions, Culture, and Ecology* 17(2): 95–102.

Lane, J. 2017. *Anthropocene Blues: Poems*. Macon, Georgia: Mercer University Press.

Langston, N. 2010. *Toxic Bodies: Hormone Disruptors and the Legacy of DES*. New Haven: Yale University Press.

Latour, B. 2014. "Agency at the Time of the Anthropocene." *New Literary History* 45(1): 1–18, 2014.

Lenton, T., J. Rockström, O. Gaffney, et al. 2019. "Climate Tipping Points – Too Risky to Bet Against." *Nature* 575(28): 592–595.

Leslie, H. A., M. J. M. van Velzen, S. H. Brandsma, et al. 2022. "Discovery and Quantification of Plastic Particle Pollution in Human Blood." *Environmental International* 163: 1–8. www.sciencedirect.com/science/article/pii/S0160412 022001258.

Liboiron, M. 2018. "How Plastic Is a Function of Colonialism." *Teen Vogue*. December 21, 2018. www.teenvogue.com/story/how-plastic-is-a-function-of-colonialism.

Lieu, B. 2015. "Plastic." A Poem in C. S. Perez, "The Poetry of Plastic." *The Hawaii Independent*. October 21, 2015. www.thehawaiiindependent.com/story/the-poetry-of-plastic/.

"Life Below Water." Global Coral Reef Monitoring Network of the International Coral Reef Initiative. www.unep.org/interactive/status-world-coral-reefs/.

Llywelyn, M. 1993 *The Elementals*. New York: TOR.

Lozano, K. 2020. "Kamilo Beach Hawaii – 'Plastic Beach.'" The Beach Blog. December 1, 2020. https://thebeach.kikipatsch.cikeys.com/ecology/kamilo-beach-hawaii-plastic-beach/.

Luisetti, F. 2022. "Earth Beings." Unruly Natures Project – A Transdisciplinary Collaborative Research Project on "Earth-Beings" Initiated by F. Luisetti and F. Gradin. May 17, 2022. https://unrulynatures.ch/Earth-Beings.

Majewska-Güde, K. 2021. "Understanding with Water: Hydro-Art in Osieki (1973)." *Przeglad Kulturoznawczy* (2)48: 356–374.

Martinez, A. R. 2011. "Swirling Seas of Plastic Trash: Long-Lasting Oceanic Garbage Threatens Marine Life." *Science News Explores*. June 22, 2011. www.sciencenewsforstudents.org/article/swirling-seas-plastic-trash.

Masson-Delmotte, V., H.-O. Pörtner, P. Zhai, eds. *IPCC. 2018: Global Warming of 1.5°C*. An IPCC Special Report. pp. 3–559. www.ipcc.ch/site/assets/uploads/sites/2/2019/06/SR15_Full_Report_High_Res.pdf.

McGovan, J. 2022. "Why Scientists Are Rallying to Save Ponds." *The Revelator* November 7, 2022. https://therevelator.org/ponds-biodiversity-climate/.

McKinley, E. 2023. "Foreword: Ocean Space and the Marine Social Sciences." In K. Peters, J. Anderson, A. Davies, and P. Steinberg, eds. *The Routledge Handbook of Ocean Space*. New York: Routledge, pp. xxi–xxiii.

McMillin, T. S. *Strange Waters*. 2022. Digital Book. https://tsmcmillin.com/scalar/strange-waters/index.

Mentz, S. 2009a. "Toward a Blue Cultural Studies: The Sea, Maritime Culture, and Early Modern English Literature." *Literature Compass* 6(5): 997–1013.

Mentz, S. 2009b. *At the Bottom of Shakespeare's Ocean*. London: Bloomsbury.

Mentz, S. 2020. *Ocean*. New York: Bloomsbury Academic.

Mentz, S. 2021. "Ice/Water/Vapor." In J. J. Cohen and S. Foote, eds. *The Cambridge Companion to Environmental Humanities*. Cambridge: Cambridge University Press, pp. 185–198.

Mentz, S. 2022. "A Poetics of Planetary Water: The Blue Humanities after John Gillis." *Coastal Studies and Society*. Special Issue Honoring John Gillis (1939-2021). October 13, 2022, pp. 1–16. https://doi.org/10.1177/26349817221133199.

Mentz, S., and M. E. Rojas. 2017. "Introduction: 'The Hungry Ocean.'" In S. Mentz and M. E. Rojas, eds. *The Sea and Nineteenth-Century Anglophone Literary Culture*. New York: Routledge, pp. 1–14.

Miller, K. A., K. F. Thompson, P. Johnston, and D. Santillo. 2018. "An Overview of Seabed Mining Including the Current State of Development, Environmental Impacts, and Knowledge Gaps." *Frontiers in Marine Science* 4, Article 418: 1–24.

Moore, C, P. Corcoran, and K. Jazvac. 2014. "An Anthropogenic Marker Horizon in the Future Rock Record." *GSA Today* 24(6): 4–8.

NASA Earth Observatory. "Water." https://earthobservatory.nasa.gov/topic/water.

Neimanis, A. 2012. "Hydrofeminism: Or, On Becoming a Body of Water." In H. Gunkel, C. Nigianni, and F. Söderbäck, eds. *Undutiful Daughters: New Directions in Feminist Thought and Practice*. New York: Palgrave Macmillan, pp. 85–99.

Neimanis, A. 2017. *Bodies of Water: Posthuman Feminist Phenomenology*. London: Bloomsbury.

Nelson, M. 2002. "Constructing a Confluence." In D. Rothenberg and M. Ulvaeus, eds. *Writing on Water*. Cambridge: MIT Press, pp. 15–31.

Nixon, R. 2011. *Slow Violence and the Environmentalism of the Poor*. Massachusetts: Harvard University Press.

Oliver, M. 1986. "The Waves." In *Dream Work*. New York: Atlantic Monthly Press.

Oliver, Mary. 2012. "THE POET COMPARES HUMAN NATURE TO THE OCEAN FROM WHICH WE CAME." In *A Thousand Mornings: Poems*. New York: Penguin Books.

Oppermann, S. 2013. "Enchanted by Akdeniz: The Fisherman of Halicarnassus's Narratives of the Mediterranean." *Ecozon@* 4(2): 100–116.

Oppermann, S. 2018. "The Scale of the Anthropocene: Material Ecocritical Reflections." *Mosaic* 51(3): 1–17.

Oppermann, S. 2019. "Storied Seas and Living Metaphors in the Blue Humanities." *Configurations* 27(4): 443–461.

Oruc, F. 2022. "Thalassological Worldmaking and Literary Circularities in the Indian Ocean." *Comparative Literature* 74(2): 147–155.

Ostler, J., and N. Estes. 2019. "The Supreme Law of the Land: Standing Rock and the Dakota Access Pipeline." In N. Estes and J. Dhillon, eds. *Standing with Standing Rock: Voices from the #NoDAPL Movement*. Minneapolis: University of Minnesota Press, pp. 96–100.

Ozelkan, E., Z. D. Uca Avci, and M. Karaman. 2011. "Investigation on Draining of the Lake Amik and the Related Environmental Changes by Using Remote Sensing Technology." Conference Paper. 31. EARSeL Prague, pp. 20–29. www.researchgate.net/publication/268811713_Investigation_on_Draining_of_Lake_Amik_and_the_Related_Environmental_Changes_by_Using_Remote_Sensing_Technology

Perez, C. S. 2015. "The Poetry of Plastic. Pacific Eco-Poetics." *The Hawaii Independent*. 21 October 2015. https://thehawaiiindependent.com/collections/pacific-eco-poetics.

Perez, C. S. 2020. "'The Ocean in Us': Navigating the Blue Humanities and Diasporic Chamoru Poetry." *Humanities* 9(66): 1–11.

Pinnix, A. 2022. "Surfacing Ecological Disaster: Poets for Living Waters and the Deepwater Horizon Oil Spill." *Zeitschrift für Anglistik und Amerikanistik* 70(1): 75–88.

Price, G. A.V., J. L. Stauber, D. F. Jolley, et al. 2023. "Natural Organic Matter Source, Concentration, and pH Influences the Toxicity of Zinc to a Freshwater Microalga." *Environmental Pollution* 318: 1–11.

Price, R. 2017. "Afterword: The Last Universal Commons." *Comparative Literature* 69(1): 45–53.

Radomska, M., and C. Åsberg. 2020. "Doing Away with Life – On Biophilosophy, the Non/Living,Toxic Embodiment, and Reimagining Ethics." In E. Berger, K. Mäki-Reinikka, K. O'Reilly, and H. Sederholm, eds. *Art as We Don't' Know It*. Tallin: Printon, pp. 52–61.

Ranganathan, M. 2022. "CODA: The Racial Ecologies of Urban Wetlands." *International Jorunal of Urban and Regional Research* 46(1):1–4. https://doi.org/10.1111/1468-2427.13096.

Reith, F. 2011. "Life in the Deep Subsurface." *Geology* 39(3): 287–288.

Rentschler, A., and K. Williams. 2022. "Community Engagement and the Importance of Partnerships within the Great Lakes Areas of Concern Program: A Mixed-Methods Case Study." *Journal of Great Lakes Research* 48(6):1473–1484.

Rights of Rivers Report, The. 2017. https://www.rightsofrivers.org.

Ripple, W. J., C. Wolf, T. M. Newsome, P. Bernard, and W. R. Moomaw. 2020. "World Scientists' Warning of a Climate Emergency." *BioScience* 70(1): 8–12. https://doi.org/10.1093/biosci/biz088.

Ritson, K. 2020. "The View from the Sea: The Power of a Blue Comparative Literature." *Humanities* 9(68): 2–12.

Rose, D. B. 2017. "Shimmer: When All You Love Is Being Trashed." In A. Tsing, H. Swanson, E. Gan, and N. Bubandt, eds. *Arts of Living on a Damaged Planet*. Minneapolis: University of Minnesota Press, pp. G51–G63.

Rothenberg, D. 2002. "Introduction." In D. Rothenberg and M. Ulvaeus, eds. *Writing on Water*. Cambridge: MIT Press, pp. xii–xvi.

Rushdie, S. 1990. *Haroun and the Sea of Stories*. London: Granta Books.

Savun-Hekimoğlu, B., and C. Gazioğlu. 2021. "Mucilage Problem in the Semi-Enclosed Seas: Recent Outbreak in the Sea of Marmara." *International Journal of Environment and Geoinformatics* 8(4): 402–413.

Scaramelli, C. 2013. "Making Sense of Water Quality: Multispecies Encounters on the Mystic." *Worldviews* (7): 150–160.

Schapper, A., C. Unrau, and C. Scheper. Editorial: "Megadams: On the Material Politics of a Developmental Panacea." October 20, 2020. Institute for Development and Peace (INEF), Universität Duisburg, Essen. www.uni-due .de/inef/blog/megadams-on-the-material-politics-of-a-developmental-panacea .php.

Seaspiracy. 2021. Netflix Documentary Film. Dir. Ali Tabrizi. www.seaspiracy
.org/news.

Serres, M. 2010. *Biogea.* Trans. R. Burks. Minneapolis: Univocal Publishing.

Shadwick, E. H., A.S. Rigual-Hernández, R. S. Eriksen, et al. 2021. "Changes in
Southern Ocean Biogeochemistry and the Potential Impact on pH-Sensitive
Planktonic Organisms." In *Frontiers in Ocean Observing:Documenting
Ecosystems, Understanding Environmental Changes, Forecasting Hazards.*
E.S. Kappel, S.K. Juniper, S. Seeyave, E. Smith, and M. Visbeck, eds.,
A Supplement to *Oceanography* 34(4), https://doi.org/10.5670/ocea
nog.2021.supplement.02-06.

Slovic, S. 2008. "Part I. Introduction: The Rain in Reno." *Concentric: Literary
and Cultural Studies* 34(1): 3–19.

Smith, James L. 2021. "Anxieties of Access: Remembering as a Lake."
Environmental Humanities 13(1): 245–263.

Solnit, R. 2023. "'If you Win the Popular Imagination, You Can Change the
Game': Why we Need New Stories on Climate." *The Guardian.* January 12
2023. www.theguardian.com/news/2023/jan/12/rebecca-solnit-climate-cri
sis-popular-imagination-why-we-need-new-stories.

"Status of Coral Reefs of the World: 2020." Global Coral Reef Monitoring
Network (GCRMN). www.unep.org/resources/status-coral-reefs-world-
2020.

Steffen, W., J. Grinevald, P. Crutzen, and J. McNeill. 2011. The Anthropocene:
Conceptual and Historical Perspectives. *Philosophical Transactions of the
Royal Society A* (369): 842–67.

Steffen, W, K. Richardson, J. Rockström, et al., 2015. "Planetary Boundaries:
Guiding Human Development on a Changing Planet." *Science* 347
(6223):1259855-1–1259855-10.

Steinberg, P. E. 2001. *The Social Construction of the Ocean.* New York:
Cambridge University Press.

Steinberg, P., and K. Peters. 2015. "Wet Ontologies, Fluid Spaces: Giving Depth
to Volume through Oceanic Thinking." *Environment and Planning D:
Society and Space* 33: 247–264.

Stengers, Isabelle. 2013. "Matters of Cosmopolitics: On the Provocations of
Gaïa. Isabelle Stengers in Conversation with Heather Davis and Etienne
Turpin." In Etienne Turpin, ed. *Architecture in the Anthropocene:
Encounters Among Design, Deep Time, Science and Philosophy.* Ann
Arbor: Open Humanities Press, pp. 171–182.

Strang, V. 2005. "Common Senses: Water, Sensory Experience and the
Generation of Meaning." *Journal of Material Culture* 10(1): 92–120.

Strang, V. 2015. *Water: Nature and Culture.* London: Reaktion Books.

Strohmeyer, N. R. 2020. "Our Blue Future: A Conversation with Steve Mentz." *LARB: Los Angeles Review of Books*, October 3, 2020. https://lareviewof books.org/article/our-blue-future-a-conversation-with-steve-mentz/.

Swanson H., A. Tsing, and N. Bubandt. 2017. "Introduction: Bodies Tumbled into Bodies." In A Tsing, H. Swanson, E. Gan, and N. Bubandt, eds. *Arts of Living on a Damaged Planet: Monsters of the Anthropocene*. Minneapolis: Minnesota Press, pp. M1–M12.

Syvitski, J., C. N. Waters, J. Day, et al. 2020. "Extraordinary Human Energy Consumption and Resultant Geological Impacts Beginning Around 1950 CE Initiated the Proposed Anthropocene Epoch." *Communications: Earth& Environment* 1(32.4). www.nature.com/articles/s43247-020-00029-y.pdf? origin=ppub.

Territorial Agency: Oceans in Transformation. Commissioned by TBA21– Academy and coproduced with the Luma Foundation. August 27, 2020–29 November 2020. www.ocean-space.org/exhibitions/territorial-agency-oceans-in-transformation.

Thorp, J. H., and A. P. Covich. 2015. *Ecology and General Biology: Thorp and Covich's Freshwater Invertebrates*, ed. J. H. Thorp and D. C. Rogers. 4th edition of *Ecology and Classification of North American Freshwater Invertebrates*. vol.1. London: Elsevier, pp. 23–56.

Topçu, N. E., and B. Öztürk. 2021. "The Impact of the Massive Mucilage Outbreak in the Sea of Marmara on Gorgonians of Prince Islands: A Qualitative Assessment." *Black Sea/Mediterranean Environment* 27(2): 270–278. https://blackmeditjournal.org/volumes-archive/vol-27-2021/vol-27-2021-no-2/the-impact-of-the-massive-mucilage-outbreak-in-the-sea-of-marmara-on-gorgonians-of-prince-islands-a-qualitative-assessment/.

Tvedt, T. 2015/2021. *Water and Society: Changing Perceptions of Societal and Historical Development*. London: Bloomsbury.

Üneş, F., Y. Z. Kaya, H. Varcin, et al. 2020. "Flood Hydraulic Analyses: A Case Study of Amik Plain, Turkey." *Water* 12(7): 1–28. Gale Academic Onefile: https://go.gale.com/ps/i.do?id=GALE%7CA638481528&sid=google Scholar&v=2.1&it=r&linkaccess=abs&issn=20734441&p=AONE&sw=w&us erGroupName=anon%7E6cbd4eb2.

UNESCO World Heritage Convention: "Great Barrier Reef." https://whc .unesco.org/en/list/154/.

United Nations. "UN Sustainable Development Goals." www.un.org/sustaina bledevelopment/oceans/.

Universal Declaration of the Rights of Rivers, The Earth Law Center. 2017. www.rightsofrivers.org/#declaration.

USGS: Science for a Changing World. "Freshwater (Lakes and Rivers) and the Water Cycle." June 8, 2018. www.usgs.gov/special-topics/water-science-school/science/freshwater-lakes-and-rivers-and-water-cycle.

Valandra, E. 2016. "We are Blood Relatives: No to the DAPL." Society for Cultural Anthropology (SCA). December 22, 2016. https://culanth.org/field sights/we-are-blood-relatives-no-to-the-dapl.

Valandra, E. 2019. "Mni Wiconi: Water Is [More Than] Life." In N. Estes and J. Dhillon, eds. *Standing with Standing Rock: Voices from the #NoDAPL Movement.* Minneapolis: University of Minnesota Press, pp. 71–89.

Van Dexter, K. 2022."'You have to learn the language of how to communicate with the plants' and Other Selva Stories." In I. Bencke and J. Bruhn, eds. *Multispecies Storytelling in Intermedial Practices.* Santa Barbara: Punctum Books, pp. 175–187.

Van Dooren, T. 2014. *Flight Ways: Life and Loss at the Edge of Extinction.* New York: Columbia University Press.

Van Dooren, T. 2017. "Making Worlds with Crows: Philosophy in the Field." In "Troubling Species: Care and Belonging in a Relational World." The Multispecies Editing Collective, special issue, *RCC Perspectives: Transformations in Environment and Society* 1: 59–67.

Warshall, P. 2001. "Watershed Governance: Checklists to Encourage Respect for Waterflows and People." In D. Rothenberg and M. Ulveus, eds. *Writing on Water.* Cambridge: MIT Press, pp. 40–56.

Water Resilience Coalition. https://ceowatermandate.org/resilience/?gclid=EAIaIQobChMI1PGs84v6-gIVYoKDBx1SKQVxEAMYAiAAEgI_5PD_BwE.

Water.Org. "What is the Global Clean Water Crisis?" https://water.org/our-impact/water-crisis/global-water-crisis/.

Wertheim, C., and M. Wertheim. *Crochet Coral Reef: A Project.* https://crochet coralreef.org/artscience/overview/.

Wertheim, M. 2015. Science+Art Project: *Crochet Coral Reef.* www.margaret wertheim.com/crochet-coral-reef.

Wetzel, R. G. 2001. *Limnology* (3rd ed.). San Diego: Academic Press.

Whanganui District Council. "Te Awa Tupua – Whanganui River Settlement." www.whanganui.govt.nz/About-Whanganui/Our-District/Te-Awa-Tupua-Whanganui-River-Settlement.

William J., C. Wolf, T. M. Newsome, et al. 2017. "World Scientists' Warning to Humanity: A Second Notice." *BioScience* 67(12): 1026–1028. https://doi.org/10.1093/biosci/bix125.

Williams, M., and J. Zalasiewicz. 2022. "Tending the Forests Beneath Anthropocene Seas." In D. Zyman and TBA21, eds. *Oceans Rising:*

A Companion to Territorial Agency: Oceans in Transformation. Sternberg Press, pp. 186–189.

Williams, R. 2013. *The Fisherman of Halicarnassus.* London: Bristol Book Publishing.

Wilson, G., and D. M. Lee. 2019. "Rights of Rivers Enter the Mainstream." *The Ecological Citizen* 2(2): 183–187.

Winkiel, L. 2019. "Introduction." *English Language Notes* 57(1):1–10.

Wolff, D., and D. Peteet. 2022. "Why a Marsh?" *Places Journal.* May 2022. https://placesjournal.org/article/the-deep-history-and-uncertain-future-of-a-marsh-on-the-hudson/?cn-reloaded=1.https://doi.org/10.22269/220517.

Woolway, R. I., C. Albergel, T. L. Frölicher, and M. Perroud. 2022. "Severe Lake Heatwaves Attributable to Human-Induced Global Warming." *Geophysical Research Letters* 49(4): 1–10.

Woolway, R. I., S. Sharma, and J. P. Smol. 2022. "Lakes in Hot Water: The Impacts of a Changing Climate on Aquatic Ecosystems." *BioScience* 72(11): 1050–1061.

Yaeger, P. 2010. "Editor's Column: Sea Trash, Dark Pools, and the Tragedy of the Commons." *PMLA* 125(3): 523–545.

York, A. 2018. "Marine Biogeochemical Cycles in a Changing World." *Nature Reviews Microbiology* 16(259). https://doi.org/10.1038/nrmicro.2018.40.

Zalasiewicz, J., and M. Williams. 2014. *Ocean Worlds: The Story of Seas on Earth and Other Planets.* Oxford: Oxford University Press.

Zhong, G., and X. Peng. 2021. "Transport and Accumulation of Plastic Litter in Submarine Canyons – The Role of Gravity Flows." *Geology* 49(5): 581–586.

Zylinska, J. 2021. "Hydromedia: From Water Literacy to the Ethics of Saturation." In M. Jue and R. Ruiz, eds. *Saturation: An Elemental Politics.* Durham: Duke University Press, pp. 45–69.

Acknowledgments

My special thanks go to Serenella Iovino for encouraging me to write this book.

To the Aegean Sea and the Dardanelles where my parents and I come from, and to Michael who loves swimming in the Aegean Sea

Cambridge Elements ☰

Environmental Humanities

Louise Westling

University of Oregon

Louise Westling is an American scholar of literature and environmental humanities who was a founding member of the Association for the Study of Literature and Environment and its President in 1998. She has been active in the international movement for environmental cultural studies, teaching and writing on landscape imagery in literature, critical animal studies, biosemiotics, phenomenology, and deep history.

Serenella Iovino

University of North Carolina at Chapel Hill

Serenella Iovino is Professor of Italian Studies and Environmental Humanities at the University of North Carolina at Chapel Hill. She has written on a wide range of topics, including environmental ethics and ecocritical theory, bioregionalism and landscape studies, ecofeminism and posthumanism, comparative literature, eco-art, and the Anthropocene.

Timo Maran

University of Tartu

Timo Maran is an Estonian semiotician and poet. Maran is Professor of Ecosemiotics and Environmental Humanities and Head of the Department of Semiotics at the University of Tartu. His research interests are semiotic relations of nature and culture, Estonian nature writing, zoosemiotics and species conservation, and semiotics of biological mimicry.

About the series

The environmental humanities is a new transdisciplinary complex of approaches to the embeddedness of human life and culture in all the dynamics that characterize the life of the planet. These approaches reexamine our species' history in light of the intensifying awareness of drastic climate change and ongoing mass extinction. To engage this reality, Cambridge Elements in Environmental Humanities builds on the idea of a more hybrid and participatory mode of research and debate, connecting critical and creative fields.

Cambridge Elements ☰

Environmental Humanities

Elements in the Series

Printed in the United States
by Baker & Taylor Publisher Services